MERELY MORTAL?

CAN YOU SURVIVE YOUR OWN DEATH?

ALSO BY ANTONY FLEW

Atheistic Humanism

God, Freedom, and Immortality: An Introduction

How to Think Straight

Philosophy: An Introduction

Readings in the Philosophical Problems of Parapsychology

MERELY MORTAL?

CAN YOU SURVIVE YOUR OWN DEATH?

ANTONY FLEW

Author of *God, Freedom and Immortality*

 Prometheus Books

59 John Glenn Drive
Amherst, New York 14228-2197

Published 2000 by Prometheus Books

Inquiries should be addressed to
Prometheus Books
59 John Glenn Drive
Amherst, New York 14228–2197
VOICE: 716–691–0133, ext. 207
FAX: 716–564–2711
WWW.PROMETHEUSBOOKS.COM

04 03 02 01 00   5 4 3 2 1

Library of Congress Cataloging-in-Publication Data

Flew, Antony, 1923–
    Merely Mortal? : can you survive your own death? / Antony Flew
        p. cm.
    Includes bibliographical references and index.
    ISBN 1–57392–841–0 (pbk. : alk. paper)
    1. Immortality (Philosophy) 2. Identity (psychology) 3. Parapsychology. I. Flew, Antony, 1923– Logic of mortality. II. Title

BD421 .F54 2000
129—dc21   00–045842
                                                                              CIP

Printed in the United States of America on acid-free paper

Contents

Preface

This book is based on my Gifford Lectures delivered in the University of St Andrews during the Michaelmas Term of the academic year 1986-7. But preparations began in the late forties, while I was still a graduate student: the thesis for my never completed B.Phil. was to be on 'Personal Identity'. Next, as the Bibliography below will make clear, several of my earlier publications were in this same area. So in 1963, when I was invited to give Gavin David Young Lectures in the University of Adelaide, I took that as an opportunity to write at rather greater length on 'The Presuppositions of Immortality'. Most of the substance of those lectures found its way into print either in the long Introduction or in the other pieces of editorial material for *Body, Mind and Death* (Flew 1964). During the remainder of the sixties, and throughout the seventies, I was working almost entirely in very different areas. I reverted to present topics only in reviews, and in occasional discussion notes; notes either provoked by fresh articles on problems of personal identity or else prompted by what seemed to me to be misinterpretations of parapsychological evidence.

But I have never abandoned the intention, proclaimed so long ago in a rash and premature parenthesis (Flew 1953, p. 3), to write a full book on *The Logic of Mortality*. I believe that it was while I was working on a B.Phil. thesis in 1948 that the thought first crossed my mind that, if I were ever to be invited to give Gifford Lectures, that might be their subject. Then, Pringle-Pattison's was the most recent set to be devoted entirely to *The Idea of Immortality* (1922).

Although the questions of survival, and even of survival for ever, gain no explicit mention in the definition of 'Natural Theology' provided in Lord Gifford's will, it has surely been usual to regard these questions, in the form of arguments for or against the natural immortality of the human soul, as proper parts of the business of that discipline? No doubt – to quote that definition – this is mainly because of their perceived relevance to 'Knowledge of the Relations which men and the whole universe bear to Him, the Knowledge of the Nature and Foundation of Ethics or Morals, and of all Obligations and Duties thence arising'.

It was remarkable, therefore, although I cannot suggest any moral to be drawn, that this subject had already for more than a quarter of a century been neglected by Pringle-Pattison's successors. More remarkable still, this neglect apparently continued till 1983, the year in which my Keele successor Richard Swinburne began his Gifford Lectures in the University of Aberdeen. The final chapter of *The Evolution of the Soul*, the first book to result from these lectures, does discuss 'The Future of the Soul'. Unfortunately, as a result of a change of Editors at *Philosophical Books*, my own copy reached me only after I had begun what were intended to be final revisions of *The Logic of Mortality*. Nevertheless, had Swinburne developed any criticisms of my work in this area, I should have felt bound to delay publication until such time as I was able to incorporate a careful response to that criticism. But, since he did not, perhaps my comments upon his latest work may reasonably be deferred.

It remains only first to confess two eccentricities and then to repay certain debts of gratitude. The more trivial of these eccentricities is to treat 'apriori' and 'aposteriori' as single, unitalicized, English words: it is high time and overtime to assimilate and naturalize two useful immigrant expressions; first introduced, it seems, as long ago as 1710, in Berkeley's *Principles*. Less trivially, although standard translations of Plato, Descartes and others are listed in the Bibliography, I have from time to time, without giving particular notice, taken the liberty of making what seemed to me minor improvements. (I have, for instance, yet to meet a student who had ever come across the egregious word 'paralogism' before encountering it in the Haldane and

Ross translation of *A Discourse on the Method*.)

The first debt is to the University of St Andrews, both for inviting me to deliver Gifford Lectures and for making me so welcome during my time in what must be the most enchanting of all small Scottish seaside burghs. (My only regret is that, because my wife was unable to join me there, I spent too much of the six weeks outside the East Neuk.) The second debt, is, as always, to library staff: in this case not only, and most recently, to those in Reading but also, and much earlier, to those in Calgary, Keele, Aberdeen, and Oxford. We academics should never forget that support staff, and above all library staff, are essential to the research and teaching business of a university. And, finally, my thanks again, as so often before, to Joan Morris. She transformed legible but unlovely manuscript into typescript appearing always so very much better than perhaps it was.

Antony Flew

How swiftly it dries,
The dew on the garlic-leaf,
The dew that dries so fast
Tomorrow will fall again.
But he whom we carry to the grave
Will never more return.

Chinese song, sung,
the translator tells us,
only at the burial of kings and princes.
A. Waley, *170 Chinese Poems* (1918), p. 38

Introduction

Merely Mortal? Can You Survive Your Own Death? is the second edition of a work originally published in England in 1987 under the title *The Logic of Mortality*. The words have to be 'Can you' rather than 'Do you', for the latter would have suggested that no account had been taken of the enormous and universally familiar initial obstacle which has somehow to be overcome or circumvented by any doctrine of personal survival or — *a fortiori* — of personal immortality. In the ordinary, everyday understandings of the words involved, to say that someone survived death is to contradict yourself; while to assert that all of us live forever is to assert a manifest falsehood, the flat contrary of a universally known truth: namely, the truth that all human beings are mortal. For when, after some disaster, the 'dead' and the 'survivors' have both been listed, what logical space remains for a third category?

All those who have propounded doctrines of human survival or — *a fortiori* — of human immortality have indicated ways in which, they believed, that enormous initial obstacle might be overcome or circumvented. Of these ways by far the most commonly favoured is what is here described — in deference to its two greatest protagonists — as the Platonic-Cartesian Way.

This way has many variations, but the common theme is that the individual person is somehow to be identified with his or her mind or soul. These putative entities are conceived — or, as I would say, misconceived — as immaterial and consequently unobservable substances that can and, at death, *do* secretly detach themselves from the bodies in which they were formerly resident and of which they were formerly in control. This is the Way presupposed in the first definition of the word 'death' provided by Samuel Johnson in his *Dictionary of the English Language*: 'The extinction of life, the departure of the soul from the body.'

The word 'substance' and its equivalent expression, 'subsistent being', are in the present context employed in a peculiar philosophers' sense. That sense is perhaps most effectively explained with the help of two references to the works of Lewis Carroll. In *Alice's Adventures in Wonderland* we can read of Alice's dealings with the cat who kept appearing and disappearing so suddenly that it made her quite giddy. In response to her consequent protest, 'it vanished quite slowly, beginning with the end of the tail, and ending with the grin, which remained sometime after the rest of it had gone' (Carroll 1865, chap. 6 p. 67). The absurdity here arises from the fact that 'grin' is not a word for a substance. It makes no sense to talk of grins occurring without the faces of which grins constitute one possible kind of configuration.

In *Through the Looking Glass* the Red Queen orders Alice to 'try another subtraction sum. Take a bone from a dog: what remains?' Alice considered. 'The bone wouldn't remain, of course, if I took it — and the dog wouldn't; it would come to bite me — and I'm sure I shouldn't remain".' So Alice reasonably thinks that nothing would remain. But the Red Queen characteristically insists that Alice is 'wrong as usual . . . the dog would lose its temper, wouldn't it? . . . Then if the dog went away its temper would remain!' (Carroll 1872, chap. 2 pp. 232–3).

Here again the absurdity arises from mistaking a word — in this case the word 'temper' — to be a word for a kind of substance, which it is not. The truth is that to say that people lost or controlled their tempers is to say something about the behaviour of the people in question. It is not to say something about members of a kind of objects which, though admittedly peculiar, might nevertheless be intelligibly said to have been lost or found as books or pens or keys or members of any other kind of domestic things may intelligibly be said to have been lost or found.

From this consideration of Carroll's instructive nonsense it should by now have become clear that the words 'mind', 'soul' and 'personality' are in their everyday employments not to be construed as words for what philosophers call substances or subsistent beings. For to construe the question whether she has a mind of her own, or the assertion that he is a mean-souled man, as a question, or as an assertion about putative immaterial substances, is like taking the Red Queen's dog's loss of temper as if this was on all fours with his loss of his bone; or like looking for the grin remaining after the Cheshire Cat has vanished. The truth is that questions about someone's mind or someone's soul are questions about the behaviour and, in the broadest sense, the thoughts of the people in question. So we might be tempted here to give the last word to the incorrigible Thomas Hobbes. In Chapter 5 of his *Leviathan* he declared: 'If a man talks to me of "a round quadrangle"; or "accidents of bread in cheese"; or "immaterial substances"; . . . I should not say he was in error, but that his words were without meaning: that is to say, absurd.'

This would perhaps be rather too hasty, and in the strictest sense too prejudiced. For the extreme and apparently intractable difficulties of formulating an in principle falsifiable survival hypothesis that is not already known to be false have scarcely ever been recognised; so few, if any, really strenuous efforts have ever been made to do it. The problem is, in the first place, to excogitate a method by which hypothesised immaterial surviving subjects might be identified in separation from the flesh and blood creatures with which they had, it is supposed, previously been intimately connected. After that the second problem is to think up some method by which such separated immaterial surviving subjects might, after what the lawyers call an affluxion of time, be reidentified as the same separated immaterial surviving objects.

The first part of the problem is rarely, if ever, faced at all. It is simply assumed that supposedly surviving souls are identifiable as the souls of the flesh-and-blood people whose souls they supposedly were. As for the second part, it is claimed that particular hypothesised surviving subjects at time two could remember that they were one and the same as particular hypothesised surviving subjects at time one. To this the decisive objection is that veridical memory presupposes and therefore cannot constitute personal identity. For when I claim to remember doing that, what I am claiming to remember is that I am the same flesh-and-blood creature as did that, that this same flesh-and-blood creature existed continuously between the date of the action remembered and the date of the remembering of it. So what could be the content of the kind of identity presupposed in the putative rememberings of these hypothesised substantial but immaterial surviving subjects?

It is remarkable that Bertrand Russell appears never to have addressed or even recognised this problem. For he once famously maintained that:

All the questions which have what is called a human interest — such, for example, as the question of a future life — belong, at least in theory, to special sciences and are capable, at least in theory, of being decided by empirical evidence . . . philosophy cannot hope to appeal to any except those who have the wish to understand, to escape from intellectual bewilderment . . . it does not offer, or attempt to offer, a solution to the problem of human destiny. . ." (1992, p. 28).

The passage quoted above comes from a book entitled *Our Knowledge of the External World*. This gives us a clue to the reason why even Russell failed even to recognise the problems of formulating a coherent and in principle falsifiable survival hypothesis, and in consequence believed that there was room for future scientific investigations before the question of a future life could be accounted solved. The reason was that he, like almost all other major philosophers since the publication in 1637 of Descartes's *Discourse on the Method*, uncritically accepted as the only proper starting point for epistemological investigations the position that Descartes had reached by the beginning of the second paragraph of Part IV of that work. In the first Descartes had argued that he must

reject as if it were absolutely false everything about which I could suppose there was the least doubt, in order to see if after that there remained anything which I believed which was entirely indubitable. So, on the grounds that our senses sometimes deceive us, I wanted to suppose that there was not anything corresponding to what they make us imagine. And, because some men make mistakes in reasoning — even with regard to the simplest matters of geometry — and fall into fallacies, I judged that I was as much subject to error as anyone else, and I rejected as unsound all the reasonings which I had hitherto taken for demonstrations. Finally, taking account of the fact that all the same experiences which we have when we are awake can also come to us when we are asleep without there being one of them which is veridical, I resolved to pretend that everything which had ever entered into my mind was no more veridical than the illusions of my dreams.

Then, in the second paragraph, Descartes continues:

Next I examined carefully what I was and I saw that I could suppose that I had no body and that there was no world or place where I was, but that I could not by the same token suppose that I did not exist. On the contrary, from the very fact that I was thinking to doubt the truth of other things it followed very evidently and very certainly that I was existing. On the other hand, granted only that I had ceased to think, while all the rest of what I had imagined had been the case, I had no reason to believe that I had existed. From this I knew that I was a substance the whole essence or nature of which simply was to think; and which, to exist, needs no place and has no dependence on any material thing. Consequently I, that is to say my mind — what makes me what I am — am entirely distinct from the body; and, furthermore, the former is more easily known than the latter, while if the latter did not exist the former could be all that it is.

The external world is thus for all of us — at least when we are on our supposedly best philosophical behaviour — everything, including our own bodies, apart from our incorporeal, substantial, and possibly immortal souls.

* * *

There are some misleading statements in the first edition of *Merely Mortal?* that I must take this first opportunity to correct. Thus in Chapter 4 I attempted 'to bring out what is logically involved in agency and choice, and to show that and how we can know, both that we do often act, and that in our actions we necessarily cannot be totally determined by physical necessities' (p. 63). From this at the end of Chapter 5 I drew the further conclusion that the Universe cannot be completely deterministic (pp. 86–7).

I now believe that this inference was invalid, and resulted from a misinterpretation of the expression 'could have done otherwise' as applied to agents and their conduct. That expression is surely to be understood as indicating only the defining difference between those bodily movements that are under the control of the persons whose bodily movements they are and those that are not under his or her control. It should certainly not be seen, as I was then mistakenly seeing it, as carrying the indeterministic implications that I then believed it did.

But once this is realised, that realisation itself does carry formidable theological implications. For if we all are creatures of a Creator in any Judaeo-Christian or Islamic understanding, then, as the ultimate sustaining cause of everything that exists or happens within the supposedly created Universe, God must necessarily make us the various individual people who we are and who, confronted inescapably with choices to be made, do in fact choose as we do choose. Such a God must therefore, by the hypothesis, be the ultimately responsible necessitating cause of everything; and everything means *everything*, including all those sins for which unforgiven sinners are to be punished with extremes of unending torture.

To this the usual indignant response today is to protest that it is only hard, unfashionable Calvinists who believe in the predestination that carries such appalling implications. The rest instead insist that the Creator endowed human beings — 'made in his own image' — with free will; thus, they believe, ensuring that God is not responsible for our making the sinful choices that we so perversely and persistently do make.

This response is on two counts mistaken. It is mistaken in the first place, because predestinationism — the doctrine, that is to say, that God determines the senses of choices for which he holds the creatures making those choices fully accountable — is not in fact peculiar to Calvin and the Calvinists. It is also acknowledged to be an inescapable implication of theism in the Mosaic tradition by Aquinas, Luther, and other classical theologians. And Islam too is as unequivocally predestinarian as Calvinism. The same response is mistaken, in the second place, because these predestinarians do not in fact deny that we are members of a kind of creature that can and therefore cannot but make choices. If and insofar as any of them do 'deny free will' it is only in some factitious understanding of that key term, introduced in a vain attempt to refute the charge that the God of Judaeo-Christian and Islamic theism must be the ultimate author of all the sins for which he so unjustly punishes his notoriously sinful creatures.

Thus, for instance, the *Summa Theologica* contains a Question 'Of Predestination' (I. xxiii, A3). There the Angelic Doctor himself lays it down: 'As men are ordained to eternal life through the providence of God, it likewise is part of that providence to permit some to fall away from that end; this is reprobation. . . . Reprobation implies not only foreknowledge but also something more. . . .' How much that something is more the *Summa contra Gentiles* makes clear:

. . . just as God not only gave being to things when they first began, but is also — as the conserving cause of being — the cause of their being as long as they last . . . so He also not only gave things their operative powers when they were first created, but is also always the cause of these in things. Hence if this divine influence stopped every operation would stop. Every operation, therefore, of anything is traced back to Him as its cause. (Book III, chap. 67)

This is spelt out more fully in two later chapters:

God alone can move the will, as an agent, without doing violence to it . . . Some people . . . not understanding how God can cause a movement of our will, have tried to explain . . . authoritative texts wrongly; that is, they would say that God 'works in us, to wish and to accomplish' means that He causes in us the power of willing, but not in such a way that He makes us will this or that . . . These people are, of course, opposed quite plainly by authoritative text of Holy Writ. For it says in Isaiah (xxxvi, 2) 'Lord, you have worked all our work in us'. Hence we receive from God not only the power of willing but its employment also. (Book III, chaps. 88–9).

*   *   *

Since the present book was first published there has been a considerable increase in the amount of discussion of the out-of-body experiences (OBEs) sometimes reported by patients after recovering from periods of apparently deep unconsciousness. I myself know of no one who denies that such experiences are quite commonly had.

Those, however, who challenge their significance as phenomena, supposedly tending to confirm some survival hypothesis, are often accused of such blinkered denials.

The only OBEs of this kind that have any claim to possess a cognitive status higher than that of any other dream are those that apparently contain information not normally available to the patient in question. Such patients were typically, at the times when they were enjoying their OBEs, lying apparently unconscious on their hospital beds. So if OBEs of this apparently cognitive kind do actually occur this ought to be taken as evidence for the reality of extrasensory perception (ESP) rather than as evidence for the making of explorations by some temporarily disembodied soul. Even if sense could be given to the idea of a disembodied soul, the postulation of the involvement of such an incorporeal explorer would be grossly uneconomical. For, having no body and consequently, no sense organs, any information brought back from its alleged travels would have to been acquired by ESP.

*   *   *

In the preface to what now becomes the second edition of the present book thanks were given to various people and institutions which provided assistance in its production. The only expression which needs to be repeated here is to the University of St. Andrews. For the book is based on Gifford Lectures delivered there during the Michaelmas Term of the academic year 1986–7.

Antony Flew
November 1999

Chapter One
Three Ways to Survival

Whether we are to live in a future state, as it is the most
important question which can possibly be asked, so it is the
most intelligible one which can be expressed in language. Yet
strange perplexities have been raised about the meaning of
that identity or sameness of person, which is implied in the
notion of our living now and hereafter, or in any two
successive moments.

Joseph Butler, *Of Personal Identity* (1896), I, p. 387

Butler, from one of whose 'Two Brief Dissertations' that first
chapter epigraph is taken, ended his life as Bishop of Durham,
in a period when such appointments were open only to believing
Christians. And surely he was on both counts of his first assertion
right? For do we not readily, even enviously, understand the hopes
of those warriors of Allah who expect that, if killed fighting in
a Holy War, they will go straight into the arms of the black-eyed
houris in Paradise? Can we not equally easily, if less comfortably,
comprehend the cautionings of a St Augustine – the man whom
his chief intellectual opponent, the Pelagian Julian of Eclarium,
nicknamed 'Aristoteles poenorum' [the Aristotle of punishments]?
(Some fairly representative samples are to be found in the Saint's
incongruously titled *Enchiridion on Faith, Hope and Love.*)

Of course we have no difficulty at all in understanding such
happy hopes, such frightful warnings. They both either promise
or, as the case may be, threaten that if people do or fail to do
certain things, then they will in consequence enjoy or suffer in
the future certain rewards or certain punishments. What could be

more intelligible than that? And, when this future life is supposed to last forever, then clearly the question whether or not we shall have it (and, if we shall, the consequent problem of ensuring that we shall pass it agreeably) is of quite overwhelming importance. For what are three-score years and ten compared with all eternity?

1   Establishing two fundamentals

But now, the sceptic urges, surely something crucial is being overlooked? For this future life is supposed to begin only *at or after* the deaths and consequent physical dissolution of those concerned; *during or after* the slow corruption in the cemetry or the swift consumption in the crematorium. Yet to suggest that we shall survive such total dissolution is like suggesting that a nation would outlast the annihilation of all its members. Of course we can understand the Myth of Er or stories of Valhalla. But to expect that after my death and dissolution such things might happen to me is to overlook that I shall not then exist. To expect such things, through overlooking this, is surely like accepting a fairy tale as history, through ignoring the prefatory rubric: 'Once upon a time, in a world that never was . . .'?

(i) The previous paragraphs got us to the heart of the matter, by establishing two fundamentals. One of these is that the essence of any doctrine of *personal* survival (or *personal* immortality) must be that it should assert that *we ourselves* shall in some fashion do things and/or suffer things after *our own* deaths (forever). It is this, and this alone, which warrants, or rather constitutes, what John Wisdom so correctly characterized as 'the logically unique expectation' (1953, p. 150).

From now on, therefore, I propose to speak simply of survival and of immortality, without qualification, rather than of *personal* survival and *personal* immortality. I shall thus be taking it for granted, first, that what at least primarily we are interested in is our own individual post-mortem futures, if any. 'Survival' through our children and our children's children after we ourselves are irrecoverably dead, 'immortality' through the memories of others thanks to our great works, or even our immersion in some universal world-soul – whatever that might mean – may be as much as, or much more than, most of us will in fact be getting. And it may be lamentably self-centered, albeit humanly altogether understandable, that we should be concerned about more than these thin, etiolated substitutes. But, for better or for worse, what in the main we are going to discuss is the possibility of our post-mortem survival as persons identifiable as those we are here and now. In the calendar words of Mr Woody Allen, 'I don't want to achieve immortality through my work. I want to achieve immortality by not dying.'

It is important to insist that this is indeed of the essence: both because some doctrines employing the word 'immortality' have from the beginning not been of this kind – Aristotle on the alleged immortality of the intellect, for instance; and because others, which started as genuine doctrines of personal immortality, have been so interpreted and reinterpreted that they have surreptitiously ceased to be any such thing. These have, we might say, suffered 'the death by a thousand qualifications' (Flew 1950b, p. 73). Well may the forthright Fundamentalist protest against 'that weasel method of sucking the meaning out of words, and then presenting the empty shells in an attempt to palm them off as giving the Christian Faith a new and another interpretation' (quoted in Lippman 1931, pp. 30–1).

It is also, it seems, sometimes necessary to point out that personal survival is presupposed by, and is no sort of alternative to, personal immortality: that in general, as in the particular case of the beheaded King Charles I, 'it is the first step which counts'.

Perhaps because he was himself 'giving the Christian Faith a new and another interpretation', one reviewer of C. B. Martin's *Religious Belief* (1959) – a work which discussed what for Butler were 'strange perplexities' – wanted to put down the whole business as irrelevant to the claims of that faith:

Christians believe that they are to be resurrected. They are not committed to any particular theory of personal identity, e.g. 'that there must be something that is continuous and identical in this life that will survive into the next' (p. 197), an insistence argued convincingly by Mr Martin to be pointless. Christians do not have a theory here at all. They believe that they are in for damnation or salvation, which is something Mr Martin does not consider. The notion of 'looking forward to a life after death as a means of settling questions concerning the existence and nature of God', which he seems particularly concerned to attack, smacks of 'Spiritualism' perhaps rather than Christianity. (Holland 1961, p. 572)

This evasive complacency is grotesque. Nor is it even correct to charge Martin with arguing that the thesis quoted within that quotation is pointless. For his stronger contention was, rather, that there neither is nor could be any such continuity. In short and in sum, survival is not an alternative to immortality. It is its necessary precondition. You simply cannot go on for ever if your first stop was final. It is therefore, once again, the first step which counts.

(ii) The second fundamental brought out by the prefatory paragraphs of this first chapter is that an enormous initial obstacle obstructs the development of any doctrine of immortality, or even any doctrine of the most temporary survival. This enormous obstacle is, of course, altogether obvious and wholly familiar. Democritus thought to dismiss all such hopes and fears with a single curt reference to that obvious obstacle: 'Some men, not knowing about the dissolution of mortal nature, but acting on knowledge of the suffering in life, afflict the period of life with anxieties and fears, inventing false tales about the period after the end of life' (Diels 1954, Fr. 294). Lucretius, following Epicurus, who himself followed the original atomists, develops the same immediate objection in his didactic epic *de rerum natura* [*On the Nature of Things*]:

If it is going to be wretched and miserable for anyone in the future, then he to whom the bad things may happen has also got to exist at that time. Since death prevents that possibility...we can know that there is nothing to be feared after death, that he who does not exist cannot be miserable. It makes not a jot of difference...when immortal death has taken away his mortal life. (III.862–9)

There are two reasons for beginning by labouring the altogether obvious and wholly familiar. The first is to put attempts to find ways round or over that enormous initial obstacle into their proper perspective, while suggesting that it is going to be at least difficult if not ultimately impossible to find a way which – as rockclimbers used to say – will actually go. The second is to show how questions of fact are entangled here with questions of meaning. In a nutshell the crux is that, until and unless such a way or such ways can be found, we do not have an open 'question of whether self-conscious life survives physical death', a question to pass to the scientists, to be 'decided by empirical evidence'. (The phrases quoted in the previous sentence came from an invitation to participate in a conference on 'Issues of Consciousness and Survival', held in Washington, DC, during October 1985.)

We do not at this stage have an open question since, in the most ordinary senses of the words employed, the two sentences 'We all of us survive death', and 'We all of us live for ever', respectively, assert a self-contradiction and deny one of the most undisputatiously established of all contingent generalizations. The former is self-contradictory because we use the words 'death' and 'survival' and their derivatives in such a way that the classification of the crew of a torpedoed ship into Dead and Survivors is both exclusive and exhaustive: every member of the crew, that is to say, must (logical 'must') have either died or survived; and no member of the crew could (logical 'could') have both died and survived. The latter is not self-contradictory but just, as a matter of fact, plain false. For it is the flat contrary of a contingent generalization so massively confirmed that it has for centuries served as the major premise in the stock example of a valid syllogism proceeding from true premises to a true conclusion: 'All men are mortal', 'Socrates is a man'; therefore, 'Socrates is mortal.'

It is perhaps just worth making one further passing remark about each of these two sentences. Our normal, sensibly cooperative practice is to give most strictly self-contradictory utterances the benefit of the doubt. Generously, and usually rightly, we assume that other people, like ourselves, have something intelligible to say, even when they speak or write in incorrect ways. We therefore attempt to attach some sense even to expressions which are thus strictly self-contradictory. This sympathetic tendency is frequently exploited by those who are competing for our attention. Posters advertising the film Bachelor Husband catch the eye precisely because the expression 'bachelor husband' is strictly selfcontradictory. The title holds us. We puzzle over it. We ponder — perhaps to the advertiser's eventual profit — the possible nonlinguistic improprieties suggested by this linguistically improper expression.

Similarly, if we see the headline, 'We survived death!', we do not just exclaim (in the tone of voice of rigid logical schoolmasters): 'Nonsense: you either survive or you die!' Instead, curiosity aroused, we read on to learn how the death was only 'death' (in inverted commas), that the people in question had only pretended, been reported, appeared, to die; but had not of course in fact died. Sometimes, for instance, people show all the usual I symptoms' of death, all the usually reliable signs that they win not walk, or talk, or joke again, but then, surprisingly, recover and do walk and talk and joke once more. This happened quite often in World War II. Russian doctors in particular reported many cases of patients who showed the usual indications of death — the heart not beating, and so forth — but were brought back to life by shock treatments, blood transfusions, and suchlike. These patients thus survived 'death' (in inverted commas). The doctors then adapted their language — or at least the language of *Soviet War News* (London) was adapted — to meet the new situation. The phrase, 'We cannot survive death', was retained as the expression of a necessary truth. But the expression 'clinical death' was introduced as a more precise and less awkward substitute for 'death' (in inverted commas), in order to refer to the condition of those patients who showed all the usual, so to speak, symptoms of death but who nevertheless went on later to tell the tale. The expression, 'We all of us survive death', thus always was, and has remained, strictly self-contradictory.

Neither the paradoxical employments of this and similar expressions, nor the inverted-comma usage of the word 'death' in which people can be said to return from the 'dead' (in inverted commas), weigh against this contention. On the contrary, they presuppose it. It is precisely and only because 'He survived death' is self-contradictory that it makes a good headline. It is precisely and only because 'to survive death' is self-contradictory that the doctors put the word 'death' between warning inverted commas when they first had to report that a patient survived 'death' (in inverted commas); and that they later introduced the new alternative expression 'clinical death'.

The second point perhaps just worth making in passing is that the sentence 'All men are mortal' has sometimes been construed in other ways. The response appropriate to its assertive employment in these different interpretations must of course be different. Sometimes, for instance, it is to be interpreted as meaning: not that all human beings in fact have been are and will be destined to die; but that we are all naturally, miracles apart, liable to die. This reading permits the proposition 'All men are mortal' to remain unfalsified by the alleged bodily assumptions both of the prophet Elijah and of Mary the mother of Jesus bar Joseph. For these elevations would have been not natural but miraculous and, hence, supernatural. Others have read the same form of words as expressing not a would-be factual generalization but a made-to-measure truth of logic, the word 'man' being interpreted as meaning a creature defined as in fact destined to die. This reading presumably carries the not universally welcome implication that the prophet Elijah and Mary the mother of Jesus bar Joseph, always assuming that they did not die but were thus miraculously translated, cannot rate as human beings at all.

Returning to the main road after that brief sidetrack digression, we can now conclude the subsection discussing 'the enormous initial obstacle' by saying that Broad was quite right to start his lecture on Human Personality, and the Question of the Possibility of its Survival of Bodily Death by asserting: 'The question of the possibility of a human personality surviving the death of the body with which it has been associated in earthly life is partly empirical and partly "philosophical", in one sense of that term' (Broad 1962, p. 387).

By the same token Russell was wrong when he wrote, much too modestly, that 'a genuinely scientific philosophy cannot hope to appeal to any except those who have the wish to understand, to escape from intellectual bewilderment'. For, he continued: 'All the questions which have what is called a human interest, such as, for example, the question of a future life, belong at least in theory to the special sciences, and are capable, at least in theory, of being decided by empirical evidence' (1922, p. 28).

2 Possible routes around or over the obstacle

Given the undeniable and undenied fact that – in the most ordinary and obvious understanding of the terms – we shall all die, then the not necessarily soluble, philosophical problem becomes to formulate some survival hypothesis which is not already known to be false. We may distinguish three sorts of ways in which this might be attempted, although the route-finding image begins to jar once it is noticed that elements from more than one of these three can be and have been consistently combined. Let us, for want of any better alternative, once again employ the three labels: 'Reconstitutionist'; 'Astral Body'; and 'Platonic–Cartesian' (Flew 1972).

(i) The first of these three ways cannot be better explained than by offering, not for the first time, a pair of quotations. Both of these will surely bear yet another repetition in yet another context. One is an epitaph composed for himself by Benjamin Franklin. When that most mischievous of the Signers eventually died, loaded with years and honours, it was not felt proper to embellish his grave in Christ Church cemetery, Philadelphia with an inscription so private and so lighthearted. Since then the Poor Richard Society have very properly supplemented the reverent respectability of that grave by erecting a bronze plate alongside, which reads: 'The body of B. Franklin, Printer, Like the Cover of an old Book, its Contents torn out, And stript of its Lettering and Gilding, Lies Here, Food for Worms. But the work shall not be lost; for it will, as he believ'd, appear once more in a new and more elegant Edition Corrected and improved By the Author.'

The second quotation comes from the Koran. As usual it is Allah speaking: 'Thus they shall be rewarded: because they disbelieved our revelations and said ''When we are turned to bones and dust shall we be raised to life?'' Do they not see that Allah, who has created the heavens and the earth, has power to create their like? Their fate is preordained beyond all doubt. Yet the wrongdoers persist in unbelief' (p. 234).

Against any attempt to make a route of this kind around or over the 'enormous initial obstacle' there is a simple and surely decisive blocking move. Obvious though this move is, at least once it has been made, it is nevertheless remarkable how rarely it has been or is pressed. Let us christen it the Replica Objection.

Certainly Allah the omnipotent must have 'power to create their like'. But in making Allah talk in these precise terms of what He might indeed choose to do, the Prophet was speaking truer than he himself appreciated. For thus to produce even the most indistinguishably similar object after the first one has been totally destroyed must be to produce, not the same object again, but a replica. To punish or to reward a replica, reconstituted on Judgement Day, for the sins or the virtues of the old Antony Flew dead and cremated, perhaps long years before, is as inept and as unfair as it would be to reward or to punish one identical twin for what was in fact done by the other. Again and similarly, the Creator might very well choose to issue a Second Edition – 'Corrected and improved by the Author' – of Benjamin Franklin. But that Second Edition, however welcome, would by the same token not be the original Signer. The force of this Replica Objection is all the greater, and all the more decisive, in as much as the 'new . . . edition' and 'their like' are both to be the creations of a quasi-personal, rewarding and punishing, Creator; not just things which occur unintended.

Whether or not St Augustine and other Fathers and Doctors of the Christian Church ever themselves felt this force, there is no doubt but that many of them did make claims which might be thought to go some way to meet it. Thus in chapter 89 of the handbook mentioned earlier, St Augustine's *Enchiridion on Faith, Hope and Love*, we read:

But just as if a statue of some soluble metal were either melted by fire, or broken into dust, or reduced to a shapeless mass, and a sculptor wished to restore it from the same quantity of metal, it would make no difference to the completeness of the work what part of the statue any given particle of the statue was put into, as long as the restored statue contained all the material of the original one; so God, the Artificer of marvellous and unspeakable power, shall with marvellous and un- speakable rapidity restore our body, using up the whole material of which it originally consisted.

On the other hand, both here and elsewhere, St Augustine makes claims about the corrections and improvements to be made 'By the Author' which are bound to increase the difficulty of identi- fying resurrection Replicas with people who previously lived and died on Planet Earth. Thus in chapter 87 of the same handbook we are told in particular that 'other births, which. . . because they are very much deformed, are called *monstrosities*, shall at the resurrection be restored to the normal shape of man'; while in chapter 90 we find the general contention that 'assuredly nothing that is unseemly shall be; but whatever shall be there shall be graceful and becoming'. Then in *The City of God* St Augustine reveals: 'As for St Paul's words of the measure of the fullness of Christ. . . the meaning is that all should arise neither younger nor older but just of that age whereat Christ himself suffered and rose again' (XXII.xv).

With St Thomas Aquinas it is different. For, although he is as insistent as Augustine that at the Resurrection the resurrected will have to have the same bodies, he does take note of the Replica Objection, and appreciates that it is powerful and to the point. Thus, in the *Summa theologica*, in the Question 'Of the conditions of those who rise again, and first of their identity', Article 1 asks 'Whether in the Resurrection the soul will be reunited with the same identical body?', and returns an emphatic affirmative answer: 'On this point the philosophers erred and certain modern heretics err. . . they held that this second union was not with the selfsame body that was laid aside in death, but with another, sometimes of the same and sometimes of a different species.' To the faithless modern the most compelling argument comes in the concluding sentence: '. . . if it be not the same body which the soul resumes, it will not be a resurrection, but rather the assuming of a new body' (III Supp. 79 A1).

The Replica Objection had of course been put by mortalists in

the Ancient World. Lucretius, for instance, after disposing of
another argument, continues: 'Nor, even if the Ages should after
death gather together a second time our matter arranged as it is
now, . . . still it would not concern us at all that this had happened
. . . (III, 847–50). In Aquinas, Article 2 under the same Question
considers 'Whether it will be identically the same man that shall
rise again?' Again the answer is an emphatic affirmative. Here
Objection 4 begins: 'The matter of a statue ranks higher than the
matter of man does in man. . .' It concludes: 'But if a statue is
remade from the same brass, it will not be the same identically.
Therefore much less will it be identically the same man if he be
reformed from the same ashes.'

The Reply to this Objection allows that with a replica of a bronze
statue it would go through: 'But man's form, namely the soul,
remains after the body has perished; wherefore the comparison
fails.' On this key issue the usually Aristotelian Aquinas becomes
as much a Platonist as the usually Platonizing Augustine. The main
thing relevant to our present concerns, which needs to be said
at once, is that here Aquinas is in effect admitting that the pure
Reconstitutionist Way will not go, being definitively blocked by
the Replica Objection.

Perhaps I may be excused for mentioning, as it were in a long
parenthesis, how gratifying it is to me to have his support here.
For often when I have argued this objection on my own account,
without appealing to authority, it has been dismissed as factitious
and merely frivolous. This should not have happened, and perhaps
would not, if only philosophers had been prepared to start their
philosophical investigations by recognizing precisely what question is being asked in urgent, everyday, practical inquiries about
personal identity. Certainly it is, once the question is put, obvious
what the courts are trying to establish when they ask whether the
prisoner in the dock is the same male (or female) person as did
the deed of which that prisoner stands accused. It is, in the
proverbial nutshell, whether, if anyone had been witness to that
action, and had thereafter contrived to keep the agent under
continuous observation, then that witness would have been able,
pointing to the prisoner, truly to testify: 'That is the man.'

Certainly all concerned will expect that, if the prisoner is in this way physically continuous with the criminal agent, then he (or she) will be able to recall not only committing that crime but also most of the other major happenings of his (or her) life. Very rarely will these expectations be disappointed. Again, everyone will expect, as between the criminal at time one and the prisoner at time two, substantial similarities in habits and temperament; and again it is most unusual for such expectations to be more than very partially falsified.

Nor are the differences in usage between the two terms 'man' and 'person' fundamental in the present context. Persons can, of course, be male or female, whereas men cannot. So neither, in any everyday understanding, could coherently be said to be incorporeal. No doubt were we speaking of one of those comparatively modest but fairly swift changes of character which often do in fact occur, we would show a slightly better feeling for the nuances of English idiom if we said, that she has become quite a different person, rather than that she is now a different woman. But then we must not overlook that none of us would ever say that she was, in this secondary sense, quite a different person unless we were sure that, in the primary and – if you like – forensic sense, she is indeed the very same.

If we do insist in this way upon starting our philosophical investigations of personal identity from the firm ground of common sense and common experience, then we will find no difficulty in feeling the full force of the Replica Objection. We will refuse to allow ourselves to be hazed and harassed by any science fiction speculations. No replica however perfect, whether produced by God or man, whether in our Universe or another, could ever be – in that primary, forensic sense – the same person as its original.

Nor could any changes, however drastic, either in personality or in memory claims sincerely made, make someone legally (or morally) responsible for what had in fact been done or not done by another. If, however, an accused person, since committing the offence of which he or she stands accused, were found to have changed more completely both in personality and in memory claims sincerely made than perhaps anyone ever has actually so changed, then no doubt the court would, under the direction of the judge, seek some way to admit these changes as at least diminishing if not totally dissolving the burden of legal (and, surely, moral) responsibility for the offence in question. Nevertheless the questions — the two different questions, be it noted — of what we would (in fact) and of what we should (ideally ought to) say were such science fiction conceivabilities frequently in fact realized are not directly relevant to questions about the present meanings of 'person' and 'same person'. For these meanings are given in present usage, and this evolved and continues to evolve in adaptation to the needs and actualities of the world as we and our parents once knew and now know it.

By his rejection of any pure Reconstitutionist Way in favour of a partly Platonic-Cartesian alternative Aquinas certainly is not: either adopting a fully Platonic account either of the nature of or of the relations between body and soul; or abandoning something which had clearly been held by the earliest generation of Christians. He is not adopting a fully Platonic account because, as we shall be seeing in later chapters, a Thomist soul would be, when compared with Plato's, a much attenuated entity. It is supposed to be a substance, in the sense of something which could significantly be said to survive and exist separately. Yet, most emphatically, it would not in such separate existence or subsistence constitute a whole person. So it is relevant to point out that any such Thomist semi-soul, which is not by itself even supposed to be a whole person, must be exposed to all the objections which can be brought against a full Platonic soul, which is, or would be . Also, to the extent that the Thomist soul is not a whole person, its claim to constitute the essential link maintaining personal identity is bound to weaken.

Nor, in repudiating an unqualified Reconstitutionist doctrine, is Aquinas abandoning something which had clearly been held by the earliest generation of Christians. For although it is never Outright asserted, in what is surely both the earliest and the most authoritative source, I Corinthians 15, that some sort of incorporeal essence of the individual will continue in some sort of existence between the death of that individual and the great collective Resurrection, nevertheless such a doctrine may well be thought to be presupposed or implied. Thus we are told that the Risen Christ, 'was seen of above five hundred brethren at once; of whom the greater part remain unto this present, but some are fallen asleep...But some will say, How are the dead raised up? and with what body do they come?' Those 'some' get a sharp reply: 'Thou fool, that which thou sowest is not quickened, except it die: and that which thou sowest, thou sowest not that body that shall be, but bare grain...but God giveth it a body as it hath pleased Him, and to every seed his own body.' The seed in this case is, presumably, the supposedly substantial soul.

To conclude the present subsection, it is worth noting that one of our own contemporaries, who has become aware of the impossibility of providing principles for the identification and reidentification of substantial but incorporeal souls (Penelhum 1970, ch. 5), has recently tried to revive a Reconstitutionist approach to questions of survival and immortality. In a study of Bishop Butler, who did not share his present successor's contempt for traditional claims about the corporeality of the Risen Christ, this author writes:

The idea of a person that the believer has is...not of an incorporeal spiritual substance as he claims. It is of a corporeal, but one-gap-inclusive, being, that has two major stages: the first coming to a sharp end at death, and the second commencing at the Day of Resurrection and then continuing indefinitely (Perhaps one should say that this conception is of persons as beings who go through three stages, not two. For during the intermediate stage there may be *nothing of the person* in the world, yet he or she will not have ceased to exist, since the final stage is still to come. The second stage would then be one of nothingness, but not of non-being.) The unbeliever's conception of a person is of a being whom death destroys for ever. (Penelhum 1985, p. 144)

Quite so. And, furthermore, even the most eirenic of unbelievers is bound to reject the proposed distinction between nothingness and non-being as incoherently Heideggerian.

(ii) In beginning to explain the Way of the Astral Body it helps to mention cinematic versions of such notions; as, for instance, long ago in the movie version of Noel Coward's *Blithe Spirit*. In these a shadow person, visible only sometimes and only to some of the characters on screen, detaches itself from a person shown as dead, and thereafter continues to participate in the developing action, at one time discernibly to the audience and at another time not; this systematically elusive entity is taken to be itself the real, the essential, person.

We shall not insist that any such 'subtle bodies' (Geach 1969, pp. 17–18) would have to be of human shape; much less that, even after the traumatic detachment of death, they should remain – as in those decent old days they did – neatly and conventionally clad. The crux is that they must possess the corporeal characteristics of size, shape, and position; and that – though eluding crude, untutored, uninstrumented observation – they should nevertheless be, eventually and in principle, detectable. Unless they were sufficiently corporeal to be thus in principle detectable, they would not be relevantly different from Platonic–Cartesian souls. However, if they were not also so defined as to be in practice excessively difficult to detect, then no one could with any plausibility suggest that such things may have been and be slipping away unnoticed from deathbeds.

The vulgar, materialist notion of souls – a notion which Plato derides at *Phaedo* 77D – satisfies the present, studiously undemanding specification for astral bodies; and that vulgar notion surely was, as near as makes no matter, that of Epicurus and Lucretius? There seems reason to believe too that many of the early Christian Fathers thought of souls as something less than totally and perfectly incorporeal. Admittedly Tertullian's treatise *de anima* [On the Soul] would appear to have been written shortly after his fall into the materialist heresy of Montanism. But in chapter VII he finds 'in the Gospel itself. . . the clearest evidence for the corporeal nature of the soul. . . For an incorporeal thing suffers nothing, not having that which makes it capable of suffering; else, if it had such a capacity, it must be a bodily substance.' (The reference is to Luke 16:23–4, the story of Lazarus.) In chapter IX Tertullian then tells a tale of 'a sister whose lot it has been to be favoured with sundry gifts of revelation'. She is said to have testified that 'a spirit has been in the habit of appearing to me; not, however, a void and empty illusion, but such as would offer itself to be even grasped by the hand, soft and transparent and of an etherial colour, and in form resembling a human being in every respect' (Quoted in Flew 1964, pp. 91–3). All such souls must for present purposes be classified as astral bodies.

The way of the Astral Body runs between Scylla and Charybdis. For the more we make astral bodies like the ordinary flesh and blood persons from which they are supposedly detachable – in order to make sure that each person's astral body can be identified as the same real and essential person – the more difficult it becomes to make out that it is not already known that no such astral bodies do in fact detach themselves at death. If, on the other hand, we take care so to specify the nature of our hypothesized astral bodies that falsification of the hypothesis that such there be, while still possible in principle, is in practice indefinitely deferred; then we find that we have made it impossibly difficult to identify creatures of too, too solid flesh and blood with any such perennially elusive hypothetical entities. Under these and other pressures those who have started to attempt the Way of the Astral Body tend so to refine away the corporeal characteristics of such putative bodies that they become indiscernible from Platonic–Cartesian souls. But we have already seen how one of our contemporaries, who had come to recognize, as it seemed to him, the impossibility of the Platonic–Cartesian way, returned to reconsider the question of the viability of a Reconstitutionist alternative. So, if and when this recognition becomes more common among those discussing problems of survival and immortality, we may perhaps expect to see others reviewing the so long despised Astral Body option.

(iii) The third, Platonic–Cartesian Way is, of course, the most familiar. It is based upon or consists in, two assumptions. The first is that what is ordinarily thought of as a person is in fact composed of two utterly disparate elements: the one, the body, earthy, corporeal and perishable; the other, the soul, incorporeal, invisible, intangible, and perhaps imperishable. Both these two elements must be substances, in the sense that they can significantly be said to exist separately. Strictly it made no sense for

F. W. H. Myers to entitle a book *Human Personality and its Survival of Bodily Death* (1902). For a person's personality can no more be said to outlast the person whose personality it was than the characteristics of anything else can be said to survive the destruction of that which they had characterized. The second assumption, and equally essential, is that the second of these elements is the real person, the agent, the rational being. For unless I am my soul the news that it is going to survive my death, perhaps for ever, would be of no more interest to me than the news that some other part of the Flew – my appendix, for example – is to be excised before the cremation and preserved, perhaps for ever (Geach 1969, p. 22). But further exposition and exploration of this Platonic–Cartesian Way must be deferred to chapter two.

Chapter Two
Plato: (i) From Preexistence to Immortality

The fact of having been born is a bad augury for immortality.
George Sántayana, *Reason in Religion* [1926], p. 260

I wonder what I was begun for
Since I am so soon done for.
Epitaph upon a girl who died very young,
in a Wrexham cemetery

Before we either begin to engage with Plato's arguments both for personal preexistence and for personal immortality, or proceed to pursue other relevant Platonic ideas which have in fact proved hugely suggestive, we need first to say something to bring out, both that – if only in the present partly out of this world context – almost everyone makes the two assumptions which together define the Platonic–Cartesian Way, and that these two assumptions are not only remarkable but also remarkably questionable.

1   Remarkable assumptions unremarked

(i) To enforce the point that almost every discussion of preexistence or immortality is inclined to take such assumptions absolutely for granted, we cannot do better than work with a paper published some years ago in the *Journal of the Society for Psychical Research*.

The author approached the question of 'What would constitute conclusive evidence of survival after death?' with the rarely combined advantages of independent-mindedness, philosophical sophistication, and familiarity with mediumistic materials. He supposed that our friend John Doe has been on board an aircraft which has crashed in the ocean, and no survivors have been found. Our phone rings, 'and (a) a voice we recognise as John Doe's is heard and a conversation with it held which convinces us that the speaker is really John Doe...or (b) the voice heard is not John Doe's but that of some other person seemingly relaying his words to us and ours to him; and that the conversation so held convinces us that the person with whom we are conversing through that intermediary is John Doe' (Ducasse 1962, p. 401). The conclusion drawn is that 'obviously, the two imagined situations (a) and (b) are, in all essentials, analogues of cases where a person is conversing with the purported surviving spirit of a deceased friend who either, in case (a), "possesses" for the time being parts at least of the body of a medium...or else who, in case (b), employs the medium only as intermediary...' (pp. 401–2).

Now certainly this constitutes as clear and vivid a description as could be desired of the model in terms of which mediums and their sitters usually think of the proceedings of the séance room. Yet it is neither obvious nor true that 'the two imagined situations...are, in all essentials, analogues' of the seance situation. The crucial difference lies in the fact that in the case of the imaginary plane crash we know only 'that no survivors have been found', whereas in the seance case we presumably know, beyond any possibility of doubt, that our friend has indeed died, and that his remains have been duly buried, cremated, or in some other way consumed. Now Ducasse in his own way appreciated all this perfectly well. The reason why he did not see it as representing any difficulty at all for 'the survival hypothesis' is that here he, like almost everyone else when considering what is in psychical research called 'the survival evidence', took for granted a Platonic–Cartesian view of the nature of man.

This is made explicit a little later, when Ducasse continues:

Thus, because the John Doe case and the case of conversation through a medium are complete analogues, the particular kind of content of the conversation that would be adequate to prove or make positively probable that John Doe had survived the crash would likewise be adequate to prove or make positively probable that the mind of our deceased friend has survived the death of his body. (1962, p. 402)

This possibly surviving mind of Ducasse's is for our purposes – as he himself in his own fashion emphasizes – nothing else but the Platonic–Cartesian soul. For it is both an incorporeal substance inhabiting its body and the real, essential person. Ducasse proceeds:

When the question of survival is formulated thus in terms not of 'spirits' but of *minds*, then the allegation that the survival explanation makes gratuitously . . . four assumptions . . . is seen to be erroneous. For (a) that there are minds is not an assumption but a known fact; (b) that minds are capable of remembering is likewise not an assumption but is known; (c) that minds are capable of 'possessing' living human bodies is also a known fact, for 'possession' is but the name of the *normal* relation of a mind to its living body. *Paranormal* 'possession' would be possession in the very same sense, but only temporary, and of a living body by a mind other than its own – that other mind being one which had been that of a body now dead; or being a mind temporarily wandering from its own living body. And (d) that telepathic communication between minds is possible is also a known fact. (1962, p. 403)

(ii) Waiving for the moment any question about the fourth of these supposedly known facts, the next task is to raise the first queries about the other three. Certainly it is a known fact that people have minds. But this is an undisputatiously known fact only if the claim is construed as meaning that innumerable statements such as 'She has a first class mind' or 'He has now come to have a mind of his own' are true. But that of course is not to say that it is a known fact that everyone is 'possessed' by, or essentially is, a mental substance; something which could significantly be said to survive the dissolution of what would normally be said to be the person whose mind it is, and which might conceivably continue to exist, but separately.

Certainly too no one could wish to deny that people are (normally) capable of a deal of remembering. Nevertheless it would be a stilted solecism to attribute these capabilities not to familiar creatures of flesh and blood but to detachable and, presumably, incorporeal mental substances. The notion of possession is somewhat trickier and more elusive. Although it does survive as a moribund metaphor in such utterances as 'He drove like a man possessed' or 'Whatever possessed her to consent?', it is significant that Ducasse found it necessary to encase the second word of the expression '*Paranormal* "possession"' within hesitation quotes. The most which these references do for him is to provide further elucidation of the Platonic–Cartesian assumptions, rather than to show how we can all know that we are ourselves mental substances possessing, or 'possessing', our own bodies.

Now is the occasion for making a fundamental and indispensable distinction between two radically different interpretations of the word 'mind', and of such synonyms or near synonyms as 'soul' or 'self'. In one, the everyday interpretation in which there can be no doubt but that we do all have minds, all talk of minds can be translated into talk about the capacities, affections and dispositions of the people whose minds they are (Ryle 1949). To say that she has a first class mind just is to say something good about her capacities, while to say that he has a mind of his own is simply to suggest a disposition to dissent. In the other interpretation, that followed by Ducasse, this word, or these words, is, or are, construed as referring to sorts of substances usually thought of as incorporeal. Following the excellent example of those forebears who first distinguished 'funny' (ha ha) from 'funny' (peculiar), let us mark the present distinction in a similarly mnemonic and helpful way by labelling its terms 'minds' (dispositions) and 'minds' (substances).

It has already emerged that, whereas it is common knowledge that there are and we all have minds (dispositions), the parallel claims about minds (substances) must be, to put it mildly, contentious. More fundamentally, before those claims can be adequately appraised, we will need first to establish that talk of such – as used to be said – spiritual substances is even coherent.

For how is it proposed that they should be identified, and reidentified through time? With minds (dispositions) there is no corresponding problem. *The Mind of Mr J. G. Reeder* – to cite the title of a somewhat passé novel – can be identified and reidentified precisely and only by reference to one particular creature of too too solid flesh. But, by the hypothesis, a mind (substance) might lack any such corporeal possession. Or it might possess one at one time and another at another.

Nor can this difficulty be overcome by suggesting that a substance of this sort could be identified as such by reference to the phenomena which these substances might be hypothesized to explain. There are two points to be made here: one about identification; and the other about explanation. The first is that members of a class cannot be identified as such in virtue only of relational characteristics. Once we have a concept of a thingumi-bob, and therefore know – at least in principle – how to recognize an object as falling under the concept of a thingumibob, then we can perfectly well pick out a particular specimen as the one which is causing this or is situated to the north of that. But it is no use to tell us no more than that your spiritual substances are what are responsible for producing all the appropriately spiritual behaviour of what you will insist upon describing not as persons but as the bodies of persons. Nor will it do to specify incorporeality as the sole nonrelational characteristic. For that is exclusively negative: not so much an eminent and distinguishing feature; but rather a formidably comprehensive lack of features.

Put in a slightly technical nutshell, the point about explanation is that the explanans must not be deducible from the explanandum. Any theory thus deducible from the facts to be explained can only be a restatement of (perhaps only some of) those facts, whereas the satisfactory explanation has to tell us more. (That is why providing genuine explanations is an essentially creative activity.) It would be pretentious and fraudulent to offer to explain their ability to put up fine performances in their philosophy Finals by revealing that they possess first class minds, if the only meaning which you could give to your revelation was that they were able to do just that. If, on the other hand, we really had equipped ourselves with a concept of minds (substances) then a contention that these particular people were most fortunately endowed with high quality specimens of the objects of that concept would be at least potentially explanatory.

(iii) The remaining task in the present section I is to bring out how very odd it is to maintain that we are as persons incorporeal substances; or indeed, anything else but members of a sort of creatures of paradigmatically corporeal flesh and blood, individual specimens of the species Homo sapiens. For what sort of object, after all, would any of us expect to confront if we were told that a person had called to see us about something? And how else could anyone teach the meanings of person-words save by some kind of direct or indirect pointing, both at the pupils themselves and at the other people in their lives? The expression 'person-words' is introduced here to provide comprehensive cover for all terms employed to refer in any way to creatures such as us. It therefore embraces not only personal names and personal pronouns but also words for people playing particular roles — words such as 'father', 'sister', 'Premier', 'bogeyperson', 'elitist', 'referee', 'christian', (non-automatic) 'pilot', and so on; and on and on.

When, many years ago, I first began to insist in the present context upon the corporeal reference of person-words I sometimes epitomized my argument in the scarcely swinging slogan 'People are what you meet'; adding that 'it is just false to say that we meet only the sinewy containers in which other people are kept; or that they encounter only the fleshy houses which we ourselves inhabit' (Flew 1964, p. 12; and compare Flew 1950a, 1951a and b, 1953 and 1956a). Against this Professor H. H. Price once objected that we do not meet ourselves. In so far as it was intended only as a reminder of the large part played in our knowledge of persons by our knowledge of ourselves his point was well taken. It is, therefore, right to emphasize that the meanings of personwords have to be taught 'by some kind of direct or indirect pointing, *both* at the pupils themselves *and* at the other people in their lives'.

That recognition nevertheless leaves us still a very long way from any conclusion that our knowledge of ourselves is, or even could be, knowledge of objects incorporeal. Recently

P. and L. Badham in their book *Immortality or Extinction* have tried to leap that gap in a single bound. To the assertion 'that words like "you", "I", "person", "Flew", "woman", "father", "butcher", all refer in one way or another to objects', they respond with what they truly insist is more than 'a purely grammatical point . . . that the word "I" can never be so used, but must always relate to the subject' (1982, p. 7). From this they proceed to infer that 'what makes me "me" is not my external appearance . . . rather it is that I am the subject of the thought, feelings, memories and intentions of which I am aware' (p. 10). This subject, it is simply assumed, could significantly be said to change bodies or even to continue to exist . . . and to have 'thoughts, feelings, memories and intentions' without any body at all: 'the flames of the crematorium will not torture "me" for "I" shall not be there. Either I will cease to exist with my body or I shall continue to exist without it' (p. 11).

Now this, as British rally drivers used to say, is going a bit quick. In so doing the Badhams have, surely, run out of road? Certainly, as Shakespeare realized, it is primarily because we are creatures endowed with conscience, in the sense of consciousness, that we are so strongly inclined to believe that talk of our dis-embodied survival is coherent:

> No more; and, by a sleep to say we end
> The heart-ache, and the thousand natural shocks
> That flesh is heir to, 'tis a consummation
> Devoutly to be wish'd. To die, to sleep;
> To sleep: perchance to dream: ay, there's the rub;
> For in that sleep of death what dreams may come
> When we have shuffled off this mortal coil,
> Must give us pause . . .
>
> *(Hamlet*, III.i)

Yes indeed. If it does truly make sense to say that the same person might survive as an incorporeal dreamer, disentangled from the mortal coils of flesh and blood, then it must be altogether reasonable to speak of death as the still undiscovered country. So Hamlet continues:

The undiscover'd country from whose bourn
No traveller returns, puzzles the will,
And makes us rather bear those ills we have
Than fly to others that we know not of.
Thus conscience does make cowards of us all. . .

Yet in the end, after the poetic play is over, the prosaic objection must be put. After the death of Hamlet, where or what could Hamlet be? Who or what is the future dreamer – the putative he, or she, or it – whose nightmares (or should it be the nightmares of which?) the Hamlet of 'too too solid flesh' was anticipating with such trepidation? (All three available pronouns seem inappropriate, though not perhaps quite equally so; a fact which should perhaps be noted more often than it is, both in the present context and in that of theological discussion.)

How – to address the challenge directly to the Badhams – is the subject 'I' to be identified; if not always and only by reference to the sensations, desires, and thoughts of the object person who is at the same time the subject of those sensations, desires and thoughts? However could it be identified thus separately, and hence as being, presumably, in principle separable; any more than mental images and bodily sensations, or Humian 'ideas and impressions', can be identified 'loose and separate', and without reference to the people who are the subjects of such moments of consciousness?

The oddity of the claim being both made and questioned here comes out very nicely in an exchange between Crito and Socrates near the end of Plato's *Phaedo*. In that dialogue Socrates, awaiting the executioner bringing his draught of hemlock, is supposed to have proved the immortality of the soul. Crito asks, 'But how shall we bury you?', and Socrates replies: 'However you like, if you can catch me and I don't escape you.' Laughing gently, he went on to complain to the assembled company: 'I cannot persuade Crito, gentlemen, that the Socrates who is now conversing and arranging the details of his argument is really I. Instead he thinks that I am what he will soon be seeing as a corpse, and he asks how to bury me' (115C–D). A few sentences later Socrates concludes with a mild reproach for young Crito's allegedly defective

Greek: 'Make no mistake about it, my dear Crito, a wrong use of words does not just strike a false note. For it also does damage to souls. No, you must be in good heart and speak of burying my body; and bury it as seems to you proper and most in accordance with custom' (115E).

But, by the relevant standard, that of customary usage, it is of course not Crito but Socrates who has here been speaking improperly. That is why the comic poet Aristophanes was able to make fun of the historical Socrates and his associates in 'the thinking shop' by labelling them, in a way which must have struck a contemporary Athenian audience as bizarre, 'wise souls' (*The Clouds*, line 94; and compare *The Birds*, lines 1535ff.).

We have insisted at some length upon the oddity of maintaining that such familiar flesh and blood creatures as people are incorporeal substances; it will be well if we conclude the present section 1 by attending to the opposite error. Under the title 'Quominus Illuminatio Mea' *Punch* once printed (5 October 1955) five verses of which the last read:

> And consider how frightfully odd is
> The fate of a Fellow whose goal's
> To establish that men are all bodies
> While inhabiting rooms at All Souls.

That would indeed be an odd contention. But it is not ours. Certainly the word 'person' is no synonym for 'human body'. For one thing, although the word 'bodies' is in some circles employed as a dyslogistic alternative to the word 'people', the degrading point of that substitution would be altogether lost were the two words truly equivalent. Again there is a difference — a matter of life and death — between, one the one hand, 'We brought a woman's body down from the Heather Terrace', and, On the other hand, 'We brought a woman down from the Heather Terrace'. Consider the following item from *The Times* of London (3 January 1951): 'Five mountaineers were trapped by an avalanche yesterday . . . Two escaped. Two others were extricated by an RAF Mountain Rescue squad . . . Mr N. Ryder

... was buried under several feet of snow and another rescue party located his body early this morning.'

Person-words do not, therefore, mean either bodies or souls, nor yet any combination of the two; and the everyday presump. tion that people are creatures of flesh and blood is not to be confounded with either of these two different, and both mistaken, claims. The word 'I' is no synonym for 'my body', nor 'my mind', nor 'my soul', nor for any combination of them; any doubters who try a few substitutions will quickly discover this for them'. selves. If we are indeed compound of two such disparate elements, then that is a contingent fact about people and not part of what is meant by 'person' and other person-words. To suggest that it has been assumed that people are merely bodies is to reveal that, you yourself assume that everyone must be a dualist, or at least a dualist with one component missing — a sort of one-legged dualist. And this is wrong.

No, people are certainly not to be thought of as just, or nothing but, their bodies. For those expressions in this context are bound to suggest the subordinate component in a mind-body duality, an inert lump bereft of any controlling mind, robbed of all those distinctive powers of thought and feeling which make people, at least within the known Universe, altogether unique. What I am wanting to insist upon is that it is people themselves, and not any possibly detachable components thereof, who, or which, are self-moving, self-directing, thinking, feeling, unitary creatures of flesh and blood.

Nor is it right to maintain that people are something much more than their bodies; not, that is, if this is construed, as it so often is, as licensing inferences to the conclusion that the something much more is a collection of capacities and characteristics which cannot but be attributed to a substance of an immaterial and altogether peculiar kind. For it is the person himself or herself, the sexed organism as a whole, it is that and nothing else whatsoever but, who (or which) thinks, desires, feels, remembers, sees, smells or hears, and is the subject of all the many other predicates typically or necessarily involving consciousness.

Certainly various organs play crucial parts in making all this possible. Yet it is as much a solecism to say that the brain itself thinks or remembers as it is to claim that the eyes themselves see, or that ears themselves hear. So, in its only halfway defensible form, the Mind/Brain Identity Thesis is the contention: not that states of consciousness are states of the brain, or of the central nervous system as a whole; but that, when *a person* is enjoying or suffering some particular condition of (private) consciousness, then that just is for *that person's* brain and/or whole central nervous system to be in such and such a (public) physical state.

2   Reminiscence of preexistence

Anyone who has ever tried to introduce British or North American students to the Plato of *Phaedo* and *The Republic* will be aware of the difficulty of persuading persons in Christian or post-Christian societies that he was equally serious and equally committed in his arguments for both the preexistence and the immortality of the soul. Indeed his argument for the latter in *Phaedo* depends for one crucial point on his argument for the former (91C–92E). In reading *The Republic* too we need to realize that the Myth of Er in Book X is an account of just one critical phase in a supposedly all-embracing process: a process which, apparently, is to be without end: and which also was, presumably, without beginning. This Myth of Er is a myth of the transmigration of souls (in Greek, metempsychosis). According to the legendary Er, son of Armenius, every successive death and disincarnation of every individual soul is followed: first, and immediately, by an intermission of disembodiment, judgement, punishment and possibly purification; and then, eventually, by the next reincarnation and rebirth – not necessarily in a body of the same species as that employed the last time round.

(i) The origins of the Myth of Er cannot be traced with confident precision. But it must derive ultimately from some religious source much further east, most likely on the Indian subcontinent. The difficulty which so many British and North American students have in coming to terms with the ideas of preexistence and of endlessly repeated disincarnation, transmigration, and reincarnation arises from their cultural background in one of the three great traditions of Mosaic theism – Judaism, Christianity and Islam. For none of these three sorts of systems of religion makes room for an eternal cycle of rebirth. Yet we should all recognize that, whatever the substantial truth of the matter, the apriori probabilities must be, surely, that whatever is to be without end will also have been without beginning, and the other way about?

Given their common cultural background, shaped for centuries by forms of Mosaic theism; given too that the future is alterable, in some sense in which the past is not (Flew 1954); then it is not surprising that both our scientists and our philosophers should have concentrated upon problems about a possible life after death, rather than upon those of a life or lives before (not birth but) conception; notwithstanding that sceptical inquirers must rate both – to coin a phrase – equiimprobable if not equiimpossible. On the scientific side the situation appears in recent years to have been changing. Although most of today's parapsychologists devote almost no direct attention to what was for the founders of the original (British) Society for Psychical Research the great question, those few who do seem now to be as or more interested in collecting what they consider to be evidence of individual pre-existence (see, for example, Stevenson 1966).

In the Ancient World opponents of these doctrines found persuasive arguments in the linkage between the two. Lucretius, for instance, confidently contended that 'just as in time past we felt no distress while the Carthaginians were coming from all sides to do battle . . . so, when we will no longer exist . . . then certainly nothing at all can possibly happen to us, making us feel . . .' (III. 832–41; and compare 445ff and 670–8). In our own century J. M. E. M'Taggart, who had no time for any theistic revelation, was at pains 'to point out some reasons for thinking that, if men are immortal, it is more probable that the beginning of the present life, in which each of us finds himself now, was not the beginning of his whole existence, but that he lived before it, as he will live after it' (1915, p. 71).

(ii) It is notorious that Plato's reminiscence argument for pre-existence takes two forms. In the presumably earlier dialogue

Meno the premise is that we can all be shown to have, or to be able to obtain, propositional knowledge which we did not acquire in this life. His Socrates therefore concludes that everyone has always 'had true opinions in him which have only to be awakened by questioning to become knowledge' (86A). He proceeds forthwith to tell Meno: 'So if the truth of the things which for us are is always in the soul then the soul must be immortal; so you should take heart, and whatever you do not happen to know at present – that is, what you do not remember – you must try to search out and recollect' (86B).

It is remarkable, though not very often remarked, that nothing is said here in so many words about eternal preexistence, and that the conclusion specifically drawn in the text – that 'the soul must be immortal' – is one which does not even seem to follow. The second thing to notice is that Plato is never explicit about what if any limits there are on the amount and kind of knowledge which is supposed to be thus available for recollection. The enigmatic phrase literally translated above as 'the truth of the things which for us are is always in the soul' is by the Loeb rendered more boldly: 'the truth of all things that are is always in our soul'. But Plato's choice of the thesis of the Theorem of Pythagoras as the particular proposition which Meno's slave is to be induced to 'remember' makes it pretty clear that, if pressed, he would have confined his claims to truths which can be known apriori. After all, these are the only sorts of 'opinion' which he is prepared to concede capable of constituting knowledge. (Compare, for instance, *The Republic* 509D–511E.)

Once this important limitation has been noticed we are in a position to grasp both the merits and the peculiarities of Plato's argument. It is peculiar in the total impersonality of the content of such supposed memories. For what could be less personal and less individual than logically necessary truths? The contrast is complete with the claims sometimes attributed to Empedocles of Akragas (Pringle-Pattison 1922, p. 107) and certainly recorded systematically in such works as Ian Stevenson's *Twenty Cases Suggestive of Reincarnation* (1966). In that we read of people maintaining that they remember that and how they themselves did or suffered or learnt something on some particular occasion 'in their previous life' (or 'in one of their previous lives'). There is of course no word anywhere in Plato of the past occasions upon which anyone orginally acquired their knowledge of the truths which they are supposed, perhaps only with the aid of some helpful prodding, to be able now to recollect.

If indeed we were all able to remember things which we had learnt in a previous life, then certainly it would follow that we had lived before: if I truly remember doing, suffering, or learning this, that, or the other; then, necessarily, I must be the same person as did, suffered, or learnt this, that, or the other. But truly to remember it is not sufficient just to claim to remember some proposition which happens to be true. For even from the facts that I sincerely claim to remember learning p, and that that colourless proposition p is true, it does not follow that I do truly remember learning p. For perhaps no one learnt p; or perhaps, though someone did, I am not the same person as that person.

So, if and when someone actually does claim to remember learning some true proposition on some particular occasion before they were born or even conceived, our immediate response ought to be that, although the claim is no doubt entirely ingenuous, nevertheless the claimant does not truly remember learning that truth. How could he? For, by the hypothesis, the learning occurred before his own coming into being. This objection accepts that the argument from truly remembering to preexistence does go through, but then reverses it in order to develop a disproof of the premise (Flew 1975, ch. 2). Having deployed another version of this same argument in *Phaedo*, Plato there appeals to its conclusion in order to refute the suggestion, urged by Simmias and Cebes, that the soul is not a substance but a harmony (91E–92C). But that conclusion, as should be now be obvious, takes for granted precisely those two Platonic–Cartesian assumptions which Plato is employing it to warrant.

The great merit of the reminiscence argument in *Meno* is that it constitutes a first attempt to raise and answer the Kantian question, 'How is apriori knowledge possible?' This merit is concealed from those who concentrate on pointing out, in a triumph of critical acuity, that Plato's Socrates is in fact teaching Meno's slave. Indeed he is. But no one taught Pythagoras; if indeed it was Pythagoras who first proved his eponymous theorem, and not someone else with the same name. The more fundamental fault of the whole demonstration is that the thesis which that theorem proves, and which is known on the basis of that proof, is a proposition of pure mathematics. Yet the opinion which Meno's slave is induced to hold is one of those rules of thumb which Egyptian surveyors had discovered long before anyone began to create geometry as a branch of pure mathematics.

We can scarcely expect to find a satisfactory answer to the Kantian question until and unless we begin by examining the ways in which apriori knowledge actually is secured. Nevertheless something of Plato's answer was to remain in the field for centuries. 'It is,' as the *Tractatus* has it, 'the characteristic mark of logical propositions that one can perceive in the symbol alone that they are true; and this fact contains in itself the whole philosophy of logic' (Wittgenstein 1921, section 6.113). Certainly, deriving implications implicit in the terms and axioms of a conceptual system seems to be more like remembering than it is like anthing else known to Plato. Just as certainly, knowledge of logic and mathematics is knowledge of eternal truths; although that adjective has in this context to be construed as 'eternal' (timeless) rather than 'eternal' (everlasting).

(iii) The other reminiscence argument, in *Phaedo* (74A–75E), provides Plato's answer to another Kantian question, 'How are apriori concepts possible?' Here the premise is that we possess certain ideal concepts, specifically that of perfect equality. Plato's contention is that these are – though this term was not available to him – apriori, in as much as they cannot be derived from experience. For where in this world can we ever confront two objects which are in any respect perfectly equal? The words chosen to formulate the conclusion in *Phaedo* are more apt than in *Meno*: 'But, I suppose, if we acquired knowledge before we were born and lost it at birth, but afterwards by the use of our senses regained the knowledge which we had previously had, would not the process which we call learning really be recovering knowledge which is our own? And shouldn't we be right to call this recollection?' (75E).

With appropriate alterations everything said about the reminiscence argument in *Meno* applies here too. In as much as both are attempts to provide answers to Kantian questions, both fail to take a sufficiently close look at what is involved in acquiring the relevant kinds of knowledge and the relevant kinds of concept. In arguing that a concept of ideal or perfect equality could not be derived from experience of a world containing no actual instantiations of such ideal perfection, Plato would appear to be assuming that to possess such a concept is to be equipped with some sort of mental picture of its appropriate object. This, however, is not a matter into which we can inquire further here. It is sufficient simply to note in passing that a consideration of this second reminiscence argument does seem to support the suggestion 'that the experience which Plato, interpreting it in one way, would have called 'seeing an Idea', we, interpreting it another way, would call 'forming a mental image''' (Hare 1971, p. 62). In this case what survived for centuries from Plato's answer to his Kantian question, and has even been revived in our own day by Noam Chomsky and his party, is the notion of apriori concepts as somehow innate ideas.

Chapter Three

Plato: (ii) Attempted Proofs of Immortality

The specific arguments which Plato adduces to prove the immortality of the soul are, for the most part, singularly unconvincing. In one or two instances he has struck out ideas which reappear frequently in later thinkers; but at other times the argumentation impresses the modern reader as frankly fantastic.

A. S. Pringle-Pattison, *The Idea of Immortality* (1922), p. 44

We noticed earlier that today many of those approaching Plato for the first time find difficulty in coming to terms with his putative proofs of the preexistence of the soul. Such students might be encouraged were they to notice how in *The Republic* he represents the young friends of Socrates as reacting to the news that their most respected senior is categorically convinced of its immortality: ' "Have you never realized", I said "that our soul is deathless, and never perishes?" ' (This dialogue, of course, is dramatically presented as reported by Socrates.) 'And he [Glaucon], looking me full in the face in amazement, said, "By Zeus no, not I. But can you say this?" "If I do not mistake me," I said "And I think you can too. For it is not difficult" ' (608D).

1 Two concepts of soul

In the first paragraph of what must have been the first philosophical essay for many years to contain the word 'soul' in its title Anthony – now Lord – Quinton maintained (1962) that:

In the history of philosophy the soul has been used for two distinct purposes: first, as an explanation of the vitality that distinguishes human beings, and also animals and plants, from the broad mass of material objects; and, secondly, as the seat of consciousness. The first of these, which sees the soul as an ethereal but nonetheless physical entity. . .need not detain us. The second. . .the soul of Plato and Descartes, deserves a closer examination than it now usually receives.

Indeed it does. But these three introductory sentences contain two major historical errors. Certainly Plato did not see 'the soul as an ethereal but nonetheless physical entity': this view he ridicules at *Phaedo* 77D. Yet it is quite wrong to suggest that in consequence he never conceived of the soul as a principle of life, and hence as possibly some sort of 'explanation of the vitality that distinguishes human beings. . .from the broad mass of material objects'. For both in *The Republic* (352D–354A) and in *Phaedo* (105C9–D2) this clearly is at least part of Plato's conception of the soul. In both places he fails to distinguish sufficiently: between an idea of the soul as the principle of life (for him incorporeal); and the concept of the soul as the true person (yet equally incorporeal). In *Phaedo* this failure is crucial to the plausibility of his great set-piece argument for immortality (100B–105E).

It is equally wrong to attribute what is in fact a distinctively Cartesian emphasis on consciousness to Plato. For it was Descartes who first, after concluding that he or his soul was essentially an incorporeal thing, a spiritual or thinking substance, proceeded to define 'thinking' in terms of all and only forms of consciousness. So it is to Descartes that we owe the modern problem of mind and matter, considered as the problem of the relations of consciousness to stuff. In setting us this problem Descartes prescribed his own private and factitious meaning for the word 'thinking', going against the grain of all established verbal habits (Cottingham 1978b). So, almost inevitably, and almost immediately, he became himself the first backslider: in Part V of his *Discourse on the Method* his 'two most certain tests' of the presence of a thinking substance are tests for rationality rather for consciousness. The price which Descartes pays for engaging in this uphill verbal manoeuvre is heavy: he not only fails to uncover our twentieth-century problem of other minds (Wisdom 1952); he also invites the charge that he denied the possibility of cruelty to non-rational animals (Cottingham 1978a).

In Plato by contrast the soul is simply the rational, responsible agent; but conceived as incorporeal. Classical Greek possessed no words which it would be correct to translate as 'conscious' or 'consciousness'; and the antithesis of outer, observed behaviour as against inner, private thought is never made explicit in what either Plato or Aristotle say about the soul. It has been suggested 'that it required a radical form of scepticism – one which expresses doubt not only about claims to knowledge of things around us but also about claims to knowledge of ourselves – to bring the outer/inner contrast to the surface in philosophical thinking' (Hamlyn 1984, p. 164). Be this as it may. It is sufficient for now to have brought out the reason why it is necessary to speak of the Platonic–Cartesian Way rather than of either the Platonic or the Cartesian alone.

A failure to take account both of the continuities and the discontinuities here has been the cause of much confusion. For instance: although the author elsewhere made major contributions to Platonic studies, the name of Plato does not appear in the index of Gilbert Ryle's *The Concept of Mind* (1949). Presumably it is this studied compartmentalization, and a consequent failure to appreciate the novelty of the Cartesian turn, which accounts for the remarkable fact that Ryle appears never to have addressed himself directly to the problem to which epiphenomenalism and other similar 'theories of the mind–body relationship' have been offered as answers (Ryle 1949; and compare Ryle 1950 and 1954, especially ch. VII).

This problem is, or was, that of determining the causal relation-ships, or lack of causal relationships, between consciousness and

stuff. Besides epiphenomenalism the most canvassed alternatives seem to have been psychophysical parallelism and two-way
interactionism. The epiphenomenalist holds that consciousness
is always an effect, never a cause: it was this which Curt Ducasse
used mischievously to describe as The-Halo-on-the-Saint view.
Two-way interactionism is self-explanatory. Psychophysical parallelism holds that there may be constant conjunctions — that is,
correlations — but never causal connections.

Now, curiously, it appears that Ryle never found occasion to
maintain outright that there is something outrageous about the suggestion that stuff and consciousness are two substances which
might sensibly be said to interact reciprocally. Nor was this a contention which it occurred to me or to anyone else to raise back in
those antediluvian days when I was one of Ryle's graduate students. Certainly matter could, and in fact does, affect mind; if by
this it is intended only to remind us of such truths as that a person's
states of consciousness are affected by blows to his person and by
his ingestion, or by the injection into him, of various drugs. But
what would it even mean to suggest that consciousness on its own
might produce physiological effects? States of consciousness just
are states of some creature of flesh and blood, not solid substances
detachable therefrom. So, pace Hume and so many other lesser
men, it makes no sense to speak of ideas or impressions, or of any
other sort of moments of consciousness, as existing 'loose and separate'. For there is of course no possibility of first identifying a
pain or a thought or a sense-datum and then proceeding to ask
whether after all it is (or was) owned or had by someone; and, if
so, whom. It is, therefore, diametrically wrong to maintain, as Russell and others once did, that properly cautious empiricists are by
their cloth required to report: not what they are currently, in a
Cartesian sense, thinking; but only that — without prejudice to any
questions of having or ownership — 'there is a thought now'.

2 The good life and the principle of life

In Book I of *The Republic* the wholly this-worldly question is:
not whether we have had previous or will have future lives; but

whether, as Plato and other moralists would have us believe, 'it is true that the just have a better life than the unjust and are happier' (352D). Plato's Socrates starts by propounding the premise that everything has a specific work or function, and that its corresponding virtue or excellence consists in performing that function well. This granted, Socrates continues to address Thrasymachus:

'Right, then next consider this. Is there a function of the soul which you couldn't achieve with anything else in the world, as, for example, management and rule and deliberation and everything of that sort? Is there anything other than soul to which you could rightly assign these, and say that they were its peculiar work?' 'Nothing else.' 'Then what about living? Shall we say that that is a function of the soul?' 'Most certainly.' (353D)

The fact that there are two bursts of dialogue here rather than a single exchange suggests that Plato himself was at least half aware that he was assigning two very different functions to his soul. Tradition has distinguished these as involving two quite different concepts of soul: the first as the rational agent, sometimes further characterized as the bearer of moral values; and the second as the principle of life. The sole direct concern of inquirers into personal immortality is with the possible survival and immortality of the former. But, because the two are often confounded, it is necessary to attend also to the latter.

(i) When people speak of the principle of life, or of the principle of intoxication, or of the principle of heat, an alternative way of expressing what they are saying would be to talk of what it is which makes living things alive, or intoxicating drinks intoxicating, or hot things hot. Once this equivalence is spelt out it should become clear that a crucial ambiguity afflicts all these expressions. In the first understanding a question about the principle of this or that is a question about the meaning of a word, the criteria for its correct application. In the second it is a question about the cause or causes of the phenomena correctly describable as cases of this or that. We are, therefore, dealing here with two totally different universes of discourse.

Terrible confusions must result, and often have in fact resulted, from failure to recognize the difference and to maintain the distinction.

When the expression 'what makes so and sos so and sos' is employed in the first sense the 'makes' is a criterial 'makes'. But when it is employed in the second sense the 'makes' is a causal 'makes'. So we now add to the distinction between 'funny' (ha ha) and 'funny' (peculiar), and to that between 'minds' (dispositions) and 'minds' (substances), that between 'makes' (criterial) and 'makes' (causal). In contexts of the first kind it must be absurd to think of a principle either as causing something to occur or as being itself a substance, actually existing – one more item demanding inclusion in any exhaustive inventory of the furniture of the Universe. But it was far from absurd to ask what makes (causal) intoxicating drinks intoxicating. For to this question, at least as applied to all the most widely available intoxicating drinks, we can now give the informative and correct answer, 'their alcoholic content'. Nor was it always absurd to raise the parallel questions about living things and hot things, or to suggest the parallel answers, 'their animal spirits' and 'intrusions of caloric fluid' (Levin, 1979, pp. 46–7). Both suggestions were long ago shown to be false. But that is another matter altogether.

The distinctions made in the two previous paragraphs possess a continuing topical importance in areas far removed from those of our present concern. Thus Bernard Coard, in a book recommended by the Inner London Education Authority in documents circulated in 1983 to all the schools under its control, undertook to explain *How the West Indian child is made educationally subnormal in the British School System*. Although this work presents several further arguments and assumptions, if none perhaps any more sound, the central contention is that the texts and criteria under which so many Afro-Caribbean children in the UK are rated educationally sub-normal are what in fact (causally) make them to be so.

(ii) There are two etymological facts which anyone discussing Plato's treatment of the soul as the principle of life needs to know. In what Wittgenstein so loved to call 'the darkness of these times', a period in which a knowledge of the Classical languages cannot be taken for granted even among those with honours degrees in Philosophy, one essential preliminary is to state these facts. The first is that the Greek word ψυχή [psuchee], which is always rendered into English as 'soul', provides the foreign root from which Englishspeakers have grown such native words and expressions as 'psychology', 'psychotherapy', 'psychophysical problem', and so on. The Greek word does not carry the elevated and faintly pious overtones of the English 'soul'. Had translators, with little or no sacrifice of fidelity, sometimes rendered it as 'mind' we might not have had to wait till the early seventies for a recognition that Plato was the first philosopher to develop the thesis that all delinquency should be recognized as symptomatic of mental disease (Flew 1973a, ch. 11). The second relevant etymological fact is that the Classical Greek adjective for 'alive' was ἔμψυχοσ [empsuchos].

The Latin equivalents of these two Greek words were, respectively, 'anima' and 'animatus', providing the roots from which we have derived such English words as 'animated' and 'inanimate'. It should be now be obvious that anyone who is thinking in either Latin or Classical Greek is likely to believe himself or herself to be equipped with a theory answering the question, 'What makes (causal) living things alive?' After all, if living things are as such ensouled things, then what makes them alive surely must be the acquisition or insertion of a soul, a life? And to be a cause this soul or life just has to be a substance, in the sense previously explained, even though the question of what sort — whether corporeal or incorporeal — may well be perceived as still open.

In this crucial sense of 'substance' — which is by no means the only sense in which that word has been employed — a substantial soul or life could significantly, even if not truly, be said not only to preexist but to survive whatever it had animated or ensouled. Perhaps the most effective way of fixing this concept firmly in mind is by appealing to examples from *Alice in Wonderland* and *Through the Looking Glass*, examples in which the absurdities are produced by treating words which everyone realizes are not words for sorts of substances as if they were. Remember, for instance, the subtraction sum which the Red Queen set for Alice: 'Take a bone from a dog, what would remain?' The answer that nothing would remain is rejected. For the dog losing its temper would depart, while the lost temper would remain (Carroll 1872, ch. II p. 223). Or, again, what of the grinning Cheshire Cat, which progressively vanished, leaving only the grin behind (Carroll 1865, ch. VI p. 67)?

3   Two anaemic arguments

The first of the two arguments which Plato's Socrates offers in *The Republic* in support of his bold claim to know that our souls are immortal is so feeble as to make its immediate, uncritical acceptance by Glaucon and the rest of the company a dramatic weakness in the dialogue. Yet, after Socrates has said something about 'the prizes, the wages, and the gifts' allotted to the just man in this life, he asserts that these are as nothing to what comes after death; by way both of reward for the just and retribution for the unjust. In response to his proposal to recount what is now named The Myth of Er Glaucon is scripted to say: ' "Please do, since there are few things which I should be happier to hear" ' (614A–B).

(i) Here the first contention of Plato's Socrates is that for every sort of thing there is one and only one peculiar kind of corruption. For all members of any such sort its own peculiar kind of natural corruption is the besetting bogey, the endemic evil. Once it has set in it is immediately or eventually bound to disintegrate and destroy whatever it afflicts; or, if it does not, then nothing can or will. He then argues that all the various forms of vice together constitute the peculiar evil of the soul. So, since none of these is as such lethal, ' "it is evident that it necessarily exists always and, if it always exists, it never dies" ' (611A).

   The entire passage thus briefly summarized is reminiscent of certain mischievous Cambridge comments upon similarly deplorable lapses in Kant: 'This is of course absolutely indefensible, and charity bids us turn our eyes from the painful spectacle'; for it 'resembles an unskilful performance of the three-card trick rather than a serious philosophical argument' (Broad 1930, pp. 128 and 135). Definitively to dispose of the whole sad business it is sufficient to mention that a piece of wood may be totally consumed either by rot or by fire.

(ii) The second and subsequent argument is, as it could scarcely fail to be, better. Like the considerations to be reviewed in chapter four, it can be promisingly suggestive even though it is, as it stands, no more compelling. Plato's contention here is that ' "It is not easy for anything to last for ever even when it is composite and not put together in the best way, as just now appeared to us to be the case with soul" ' (611B). But he goes on to suggest that, if only we could observe the soul free of all encrustations and distortions, ' "we might discern whether in its real nature it is manifold or unitary, and what's what about it" ' (612A).

Plato never outright asserts that anything not composite and molecular but simple and atomic must necessarily be indestructible. But his curious argument to the conclusion that in the Universe as a whole the soul population is bound to be stable and constant suggests that this is what he was at least very much inclined to believe. At the conclusion of the first of the present two arguments, and granting that souls are naturally immortal, Socrates says that he said: ' "But if that is the case then you will notice that there will always be the same souls. For if none perishes they will become neither more nor less numerous. For you realize that, if any class of immortal things increased, then its increase would come from the mortal and everything would end up becoming immortal" ' (612A).

The crucial premise here is another of those propositions which have sometimes been believed to constitute items of synthetic apriori knowledge, propositions which many of the wise and good have thought that they clearly and distinctly conceived to be true. It is a collection which Hume at one stroke consigned to what, adapting Trotsky, we might call the dustbin of philosophical history. Anyone, surely, who has ever taken a second look at these two arguments in *The Republic* must be hard put to dissent from Hume's verdict in his essay 'Of the Immortality of the Soul';

notwithstanding that once upon a time a second-time Gifford
Lecturer could, in the University of St Andrews, complain that
'its arguments rest on a cynical and ignoble estimate of humanity
that has seldom been surpassed' (Ward 1911, p. 386n). That long
suppressed and only posthumously published essay begins: 'By
the mere light of reason it seems difficult to prove the Immortality of the Soul. The arguments for it are commonly derived
from *metaphysical* topics, or *moral* or *physical*. But in reality it
is the gospel, and the gospel alone, that has brought life and
immortality to life' (Hume 1742-77, p. 590). The essay concludes by reiterating a contention to which the author of I
Corinthians 15 could scarcely have taken exception: 'Nothing
could set in a hiller light the infinite obligations which mankind
have to divine revelation; since we find that no other medium
would ascertain this great and important truth.'

4 Everlasting lives and timeless Ideas

Fully to appreciate Plato's great set-piece argument for the
immortality of the soul it is necessary first to be seized: both of
the relevant etymological peculiarities of the language in which
he thought; and of the very different meanings which have been
given to expressions such as 'the principle of life'. That was one
reason for delaying the examination of that argument until
chapter three. In Phaedo, a dialogue in which Phaedo is represented as reporting the discussion which occurred while Socrates
and his closest friends were awaiting the arrival of the executioner bringing in the hemlock, Socrates begins by getting his
hearers to reaffirm their acceptance of what has since been
named the Theory of Forms or Ideas:

'I am going to try to explain to you the kind of cause with which I have
been busying myself. I shall revert to those things which we have talked
about so much. I shall begin from those, assuming that there are such
things as the beautiful itself in itself, the good, the great and all the rest.
If you grant this and agree that these exist I expect to derive for you an
explication of cause, and to show that the soul is immortal'. (100B)

(i) This is not the place to go deeply and at length into the Theory of Forms. Nevertheless there are several points which, if we are to take the measure of Plato's argument, have to be made straight away. To begin with, there are the two verbal facts: first, that the word translated by 'cause' would on other occasions be more correctly rendered 'reason'; and, second, that the definite articles before the words 'beautiful', 'good', and 'great' are not to be found in corresponding positions in the original Greek. But, in both cases, the context makes it quite clear that the renderings given above are faithful to Plato's intentions. In the matter of the definite articles it is to be noted that he very frequently constructs a substitute for an abstract noun by putting the definite article in its neuter form before an adjective in the corresponding neuter form. Thus we meet – translating absolutely literally – the beautiful (thing), the good (thing), the just (thing), and so on, rather than beauty, goodness and justice. Although our manuscripts do not make such upper case/lower case distinctions it would certainly be in accordance with the spirit if not the letter to give initial capitals to the key words in all expressions referring to Forms or Ideas.

Next come several points which are in no sense verbal. For a start these Forms or Ideas are certainly substantial. Indeed they occupy the top stratum in Plato's hierarchy of actualities. They are also supposed to be immaterial, unchanging and eternal. So they become paradigm specimens of the putative genus incorporeal substance: incorporeal souls are conceived to be members of another species within that genus. The Theory of Forms provides a ready and systematic answer to all questions of the type, 'What makes instances of this or that be instances of this or that?' The supposedly correct and sufficient answer is, 'the Form or Idea of this or that'. Since these entities are substantial the 'makes' in all such questions and answers has to be construed as being a 'makes' (causal); and the production of the instances as involving, on the part of the Form or Idea, what Aristotle was later to distinguish as efficient causation.

(ii) Once the whole company has indicated that it accepts this as a starting place, Socrates proceeds to argue that the only cause or reason why anything acquires any particular characteristic is that it participates in the Form or Idea of whatever it may be. ('Participation' here is a never sufficiently explained technical term.) But some characteristics are incompatible with, and therefore exclude or are themselves excluded by, others. Socrates continues ' "Now see what I want to make plain. It is this, that it is not only opposites which exclude one another, but all things which, without being opposites one to another, always contain opposites. These too, it appears, exclude the Idea which is opposed to the Idea contained in them, and when it approaches they either depart or are destroyed" ' (104B).

After a buildup which most readers find tiresomely protracted Socrates produces the promised conclusion with a final burst of speed: ' "What causes the body in which it is to be alive?" "The soul," he replied. "Is this always the case?" "Yes," said he, "of course". "Then whenever the soul takes possession of anything it always brings life to it?" "Certainly," he said. "Is there anything which is the opposite of life?" "There is," he said. "What?" "Death." "So soul, as we agreed before, will never admit the opposite of that, which it always brings with it?" "Most emphatically not," said Cebes.' Finally, after pausing for a moment to remind the company of a previous illustration of 'things which, without being opposites one to another, always contain opposites', Socrates charges past the winning post: ' "Well then, what do we call what does not admit death?" "Deathless," he said. "And the soul does not admit death?" "No." "Then the soul is deathless?" "Yes." "Right," he said, "shall we say that this is well and truly proved?" "Yes indeed, Socrates, most satisfactorily" ' (105C–D).

So, deferring to the schoolboy geometrician's misreading of 'QED', it would appear that everything has been quite easily done. Yet of course it has not. For absolutely nothing has been said to show that either Socrates himself or any other rational agent is a deathless, immortal individual. In so far as his present argument goes through at all, it can only be because the expression 'the soul' is being interpreted as referring to the Form or Idea of life; while that that Form or Idea – along with every other Form or Idea – is an immaterial, eternal, unchanging substance is a stipulation of the theory which from the start everyone agreed that we should take for granted. No doubt the common usage by which it is customary to speak of the immortality of the soul (singular) rather than of individual souls (plural) assists this catastrophic confounding of the Soul or the Life (as the Form or principle of life) with souls (as the principles of individuation of rational agents, of individual human persons).

Immediately after completing this putative proof of the immortality of 'the soul', Socrates, just as if he had not been totally successful in persuading himself, proceeds to repeat some of his previous contentions about what necessarily excludes what. His first subsequent conclusion is that everything which he presupposes to be imperishable and eternal in fact is: ' "Everyone would, I think agree", said Socrates, "that God and the Form of life and whatever else there may be which is deathless can never perish." ' But he goes straight on from this to reiterate and underline what he claimed to have proved previously:

'Then when death comes to a man the mortal part of him, it seems, dies, but the immortal part goes away unharmed and undestroyed, withdrawing from death." "So it seems." "Then, Cebes," he said, "it is perfectly certain that soul is immortal and imperishable, and that our souls will exist in some kind of Hades'. (106E–107A)

(iii) After this, just as in *The Republic*, Socrates changes gear, abandoning philosophical argument in favour of geographical speculation and eschatological myth. Plato does not ask us to take any of this literally and at the foot of the letter. Socrates is made to say: ' "So it would not be fitting for a man of sense to maintain that everything is exactly as I have described it. However, that this or something like it is the truth about our souls and their habitations I think that he may properly and worthily venture to believe, since the soul does appear to be immortal" ' (114D). Yet this cannot be the end of the affair. For there is more to be learnt from the examination of Plato's set-piece argument to that previous conclusion.

In the first place, Plato was by no means the last to take it that establishing his Theory of Forms, or something like it, would probabilify the actual existence of some other sorts of similarly incorporeal substances – perhaps human souls, and perhaps gods and angels too. St Augustine in his *Confessions* tells how 'having read these books of the Platonists and having taken the hint to search for incorpreal truth from them, I got a sight of those invisible things of thine which are understood through the things which are made' (VII.xx: as always the Saint is addressing his God). Rumour has it that even in our own day it was by a similar route that Elizabeth Anscombe reached her Roman Catholic faith.

Once we have indicated something which it would be reasonable to infer if we had been able to confirm the Theory of Forms, and in particular that these Forms are immaterial substances, it becomes time to insist that the protasis of that conditional is after all not true. Indeed I would myself go further, to question whether anyone has ever succeeded in constructing a concept of such an object, providing principles for its identification and reidentification through time. The crux to grasp is that Forms or Ideas, being the principles which make (criterial) their several sets of instances what as instances they are, such Forms must all belong to a totally different world from that of substances and causes. It is, therefore, a most fundamental and ruinous yet nevertheless perennially seductive error to confound entities – if we may so dignify them – of the one world with actual or hypothetical substances belonging to the other. This set-piece argument in *Phaedo* is one of the first landmarks in a still continuing tradition of such confounding.

The classical study of this tradition – A. O. Lovejoy's *The Great Chain of Being* – devotes much of its attention to the identification of, on the one hand, the inert, unobtrusive and abstract God of the philosophers – deriving from Plato's supreme Idea, the Form of the Good; with, on the other hand, the restlessly active, intervening and demanding agent God of Abraham, Isaac and Jacob. For '. . . the God of Aristotle had almost nothing in common with the God of the Sermon on the Mount – though, by one of the strangest and most momentous paradoxes in Western history, the philosophical theology of Christendom identified them . . .' (Lovejoy 1936, p. 5).

Recognizing the great gulf which separates each one of these two worlds from the other, we now have to distinguish two senses of 'eternal'. In one, appropriate to Ideas and concepts, it means timeless; in as much as it makes no sense to ask temporal questions about conceptual relations. In the other, applicable to the world of events and activities, it means everlasting. The nerve of this crucial distinction is neatly and nicely displayed in critical remarks directed against a Gifford Lecturer less frank in his atheism than the present writer:

I suspect some theologians of wishing to replace this conception of an eternal God, whose changeless duration coexists with and over-flows the duration of mutable things, with the conception of a God who is changeless because *not actual*. Surely it is for this reason that we hear so much of its being wrong to say that God *exists*; for this reason that Tillich emphatically repudiates the idea of a God who acts – who 'brought the Universe into existence at a certain moment, governs it according to a plan, directs it to an end' [Tillich 1968, II, p. 6]. Well, I suppose people can worship the non-actual as Pythagoreans worshipped the number Four; but it is excessively misleading if they claim to be worshipping the God of Judaism and Christianity. (Geach 1969, p. 74)

Some at least of what we find some writers saying about the soul's hankering after or devoting itself to things eternal has to be understood in terms of the distinction between these two radically different senses of that word. Since it has here to be read as meaning timeless, these passages have no direct bearing on the question of a future life. Even so unhesitating and consistent a mortalist as Russell could at times sympathize with such longings. Thus, in the chapter entitled 'the World of Universals' in his classic introduction *The Problems of Philosophy*, he wrote of that world that it 'is unchangeable, rigid, exact, delightful to the mathematician, the logician, the builder of metaphysical systems, and all who love perfection more than life' (Russell [1911], p. 57). And in the *Tractatus* too we read: 'If by eternity is understood not endless temporal duration but timelessness, then he lives eternally who lives in the present' (Wittgenstein 1921, section 6.4311; and compare Phillips 1970, ch. 3).

5   Plato defends Platonic assumptions

As we have seen, Plato in his attempts to prove that people are naturally immortal always takes for granted Platonic assumptions about the nature of man. Only towards the end of *Alcibiades* I, a dialogue which some scholars have suspected not to be an authentic work of Plato, can we find any direct argument for the indispensable presupposition that people as rational agents just are their incorporeal souls; and even here, as so often later and elsewhere, no question is raised about whether we are adequately equipped with a viable concept of immaterial substance. There are, however, both in *Phaedo* and in other dialogues, suggestions that some characteristics, which without instruction we might have believed peculiar to and distinctive of a certain familiar kind of creatures of flesh and blood, are in truth correctly predicated only of specimens of this most remarkable sort of substance. The most promising prospect for the defence of a Platonic view of the nature of man lies, as we shall begin to see in chapter four, in the development of these suggestions.

What is propounded as a demonstration in *Alcibiades* I is luminously simple and straightforward. Socrates opens by asking Alcibiades: ' "To whom are you talking now? To me, are you not?" "Yes." "And I in turn to you?" "Yes." "Then the talker is Socrates?" "To be sure" "And the hearer Alcibiades?" "Yes." (129B). The stage thus set, Socrates cites instances in which for various purposes people use parts of or the whole of their bodies. Since the entire script is, as usual, written by Plato, Socrates has no difficulty in getting Alcibiades to agree that the user and the thing used are always different. This given, the desired conclusion is quickly drawn: ' "So man is different from his own body?" "It seems so." "Then whatever is man?" "I cannot say" "Oh but you can – that he is the user of the body." "Yes" "And is anything else but soul using it?" "Nothing else." ' (129E–130A).

To this elegant exercise the obvious yet none the less decisive objection is that those many instances in which, quite correctly, we speak of people employing parts or the whole of their bodies in order to achieve this or that purpose, all ought to be accepted as counter-examples falsifying the premise 'that the user and the thing used are always different''. Certainly there were in Classical Greek, and are in English and other modern languages, innumerable idioms which may tempt us to draw Platonic–Cartesian conclusions. Yet, until and unless we can overcome the difficulties involved in any substance interpretation of such words as 'mind', 'soul' or 'self', we should recognize the suggestions of these idioms as temptations to reject, rather than construe them as clues to follow. (Compare chapter two, section 1(i), above.)

Nor is that a warning which was needed only in the spring of the world. For example: a recent and extremely sophisticated author wants somehow to reject unfashionably Cartesian views of the nature of man while nevertheless conceding that it makes sense to talk of persons *disembodied* or in control of the bodies they *possess*. Quite early on in what is a generally excellent book he manoeuvres himself onto this concessionary slope by choosing to say: not, given that we are creatures of flesh and blood; but, 'given that we are creatures with bodies' (Hamlyn 1984, p. 83). He then slides further by wondering 'how Bradley views the position of the self in his scheme of things' (p. 125). Even when, much later (p. 188), he offers some explanation of this peculiar technical employment of that suffix he still fails to bring out the crucial truth that no one appears to have provided any means of identifying selves save by reference to the flesh and blood creatures whose selves they are to be defined as being.

Again, after pointing out that we cannot infer directly, from the fact that 'all the conscious beings that we know of in our everyday lives are...bodily' (p. 175), the conclusion 'that consciousness must always be embodied' (p. 176), the same author nevertheless proceeds to talk about 'those embodied conscious beings...which we exemplify ourselves' (p. 176), and about how 'those bodies are the bodies of persons, they are owned by them' (p. 186). That he really does want this ownership to be construed as that of some entity separable from the thing owned is made embarrassingly clear by the following sentence: 'The states of merely physical things are not owned by anything in that sense' (p. 186). Indeed they are not!

Chapter Four

Plato: (iii) Intimations of Immateriality

Nothing happens at random; everything happens out of reason and by necessity.

> Leucippus of Abdera: Fragment 2, in H. Diels,
> *Fragmente der Vorsokratiker* (1954)

Many there be that complain of divin Providence for suffering *Adam* to transgresse, foolish tongues! when God gave him reason he gave him freedom to choose, for reason is but choosing; he had bin else a meer artificiall *Adam*, such an *Adam* as he is in the motions.

> John Milton, *Areopagitica* (n.d.), p. 702

The argument presented in *Alcibiades* I is unequivocal, crude, and explicit; although, as on some other occasions, Socrates did afterwards hint that it may be only 'more or less' rather than 'exactly' correct (130C). Nevertheless, as we have just seen, the same argument, in a rather less open, more ambiguous guise, still continues to hold some often subtle thinkers in thrall. More important by far, however, are certain hints. Plato himself seems never to have shaped them into any systematic attempts to demonstrate the necessary immateriality of rational agents. Yet these three suggestions have had enormous influence, not least upon many altogether unaware of their Classical source. (After all, as St Jerome remarks in his *Commentary on Galatians*, 'How many nowadays know the works or even the name of Plato? A handful of idle old men.')

One of these suggestions, which was to come into its own only with the new Cartesian emphasis upon consciousness, was mentioned in section 3 (ii) of the previous chapter three. It is that anything indivisible and unitary must be naturally indestructible. Much has from time to time been made of this by those persuaded that we can both significantly and truly say that every individual consciousness is a substance possessing this kind of unity (Lewis 1978, p. 118). But it is the other two which have proved far more fertile, and which deserve rather more extensive treatment.

1   Unmoved movement and acting for reasons; both supposed immaterial

In *Timaeus*, which pretends to be a sequel to *The Republic*, much is made of a distinction between two kinds of cause. One is the familiar and uncontroversially material kind, 'cooling and heating, solidifying and dissolving, and producing all effects of that sort. But these are incapable of possessing reason and thought for any purpose.' The other kind is equally familiar yet supposedly immaterial. 'For, we must insist, of all there is, the only thing to which we can properly attribute thought is mind. And this is invisible, whereas fire and water and earth and air are all visible bodies' (46D: the word previously rendered as 'soul' here becomes 'mind'). Two further key ideas are introduced now, those of self-movement and of physical necessity:

But the lover of thought and knowledge must needs pursue the primary causes of intelligent Nature; whereas all those which are moved by something else move other things by necessity. We too must act likewise. We must admit both kinds of causes, but distinguish those which, having thought, are artificers of things fine and good, from those which, devoid of sense, always bring about accidental and irregular effects. (46D–E)

(i) In *Phaedrus* we find a fuller account of these self-moving primary causes which, when they move either themselves or others, are not externally necessitated so to do. In order to feel the force of the argument put by Plato's Socrates we have: not only to remember the etymological linkage between the Greek words for soul and for life; but also to recognize that, at least to common observation, living things appear to be the only true initiators of motion. The argument begins: 'Every soul is immortal. For what is ever-moving is immortal, whereas what moves something else and is moved by something else, when it ceases to move ceases to live. Only what moves itself, since it does not leave itself, never ceases to move. This, however, is the source and origin of motion for all the other things which move'' (245C–D). But what is, because unmoved by anything else, ungenerated must necessarily be, the argument continues, indestructible. So, ''since what is moved by itself has been seen to be immortal, anyone who says that this is the essence and the very idea of the soul will not be disgraced. For every body which is moved from outside is soulless whereas what moves under its own momentum is alive, because that is the nature of soul'' (245E).

According to the principles of this argument in *Phaedrus* every single living creature must be possessed of, or possessed by, its own immortal soul. So, when Socrates goes on to expound a myth of metempsychosis we should be surprised only that so very little is said about the souls of the brutes, not that we are once told that a formerly 'human soul may enter into the existence of a beast' (249B). This Platonic suggestion that all motion has to be both initiated and sustained by incorporeal and presumably substantial souls was later to provide a key element in Aristotle's physics. It is therefore, as Soviet spokespersons so love to say, no accident that we can find in all the three great Scholastic traditions of Mosaic theism – Christian, Muslim and Jewish – arguments to a Prime Mover as the ultimate source and support of all motion. (In the *Summa theologica* St Thomas Aquinas, unmindful of the rule requiring the employment of the superlative where a comparison has more than two terms, actually writes 'manifestior' – more manifest – when he wants to insist that this argument is the most manifest of all his Five Ways to demonstrate the existence of God.)

Certainly too we need today to remind ourselves of 'the peculiar character of that Aristotelian universe in which the things that were in motion had all the time to be accompanied by their movers. A universe constructed on the mechanics of Aristotle had the door half way open for spirits already; it was a universe in which unseen hands had to be in constant operation, and sublime Intelligences had to roll the planetary spheres around' (Butterfield 1951, p. 7). Given our present interests, we also need to notice that the hesitation suggested by the expression 'half way open' is well warranted. Such souls are ill-equipped to serve as the hypothetical entities of an explanatory theory. For no one is able to propose any way in which they might be identified, apart from the movements which they were hypothesized to explain. Nor, once we have adopted this supposed hypothesis, are there any fresh and testable inferences to be drawn. *The Origins of Modern Science* continues:

The modern law of inertia, the modern theory of motion, is the great factor which in the seventeenth century helped to drive the spirits out of the world. . . Not only so – but the very first men who in the middle ages launched the great attack on the Aristotelian theory were conscious of the fact that this colossal issue was involved in the question. . . Jean Buridan, in the fourteenth century, pointed out that his alternative interpretation would eliminate the need for the Intelligences that turned the celestial spheres. He even noted that the Bible provided no authority for these agencies. . . (Butterfield 1951, pp. 6–7)

(ii) Plato's best account of his two kinds of cause comes in what perhaps is, and certainly deserves to be, the most often quoted passage from *Phaedo*. Socrates is here said to have told how one day in his youth he ' "heard a man reading from a book, as he said, by Anaxagoras, saying that it is intelligence which is the orderer and cause of all things." ' Socrates was thrilled, inferring that, if intelligence is the cause of all things, then ' "intelligence in arranging everything sets each thing up as it is best for it to be" ' (97B–C). His response to the let-down of discovering that this was not at all what Anaxagoras was trying to establish was to develop his own distinction as a distinction between the sole true causes and what are alleged to be mere pseudo-causes.

He develops it with dramatic reference to his own situation as a prisoner awaiting execution. What Anaxagoras was in fact saying

'seemed to me very much as if someone were to say that Socrates does whatever he does with intelligence, and then, in trying to give the causes of the particular things which I do, should say first that I am now sitting here because my body is composed of bones and sinews...Or as if in the same way he should give voice and ear and hearing and countless other things of that sort as the causes of our talking with each other, and should neglect to mention the true causes, which are, that the Athenians decided that it was best to condemn me, and that on the account I have also decided that it is best for me to sit here, and that the right thing to do is to stay and to accept whatever penalty they order.' (98C–E)

So Socrates concludes that

'If anyone were to say that, if I had not bones and sinews and whatever else I have, I could not have done what I thought right, he would be speaking truth. But to say that they are why I do what I do, and that I do these things with intelligence but not by choice of what is best, would be an extremely careless way of talking. For that is to be unable to make a distinction, to see that in reality a cause is one thing and the thing without which a cause could never be a cause is quite another thing.' (99A–B)

It is clear from all this that Plato's true causes are the reasons for which agents act. They are their motives and purposes in so acting. But, since it is notorious that actual agents do not always make intelligent decisions and do not always act for the best, it should be equally clear that not even the most dedicated search for such causes is going to show us that some universal 'intelligence in arranging everything sets each thing up as it is best for it to be.' It is also clear that Plato is assuming that to explain a person's agent behaviour in terms of causes of the kind which constitute reasons for acting is somehow to show that the true agent is not the flesh and blood person but an incorporeal controller possessing, or imprisoned in, that person's body. For the purpose of introducing this distinction here – contrasting such supposedly immaterial, and in a sense rational, true causes with sordidly material, mere pseudo-causes – just is, surely, to effect that desired demonstration?

Much more will in due course have to be said about such curious assumptions. For it should indeed appear very curious that so many people are able to persuade themselves that various predicates felt to be high-toned and rather splendid cannot properly be attributed to precisely that sort of subjects which are and always have been everyone's paradigm cases of their correct application.

The immediate next task, however, is to bring out how wrong it must be to identify the operation of causes of this 'rational' kind with physical necessitation. The truth is that whereas causes of the other kind, which Plato here disqualifies as causes, do physically necessitate the occurrence of their effects, causes of the present approved sort do not. The nearest he comes to saying this is when he scripts Socrates to reject the suggestion that causes of that other kind 'are why I do what I do, and that I do these things with intelligence but not by choice of what is best'. It is not very near.

It is, nevertheless, a matter of the last importance; and altogether relevant. For both those who recognize and those who refuse to recognize the reality of authentic and, consequently, unnecessitated choice have commonly believed that purely material beings could not be creatures such as we persons are; creatures, that is, who can, and cannot but, constantly make such genuine and physically unnecessitated choices. Thus, speaking in his own voice, the author of an excellent little book, *Body and Mind*, maintains, in particular: 'A brain in which there are undetermined irregular physical events, is a brain which, although acted on only by physical influences, is not at every point subject to the laws governing material things. It would not be a *purely material object*' (Campbell 1970, p. 18).

Later the same author provides a very sympathetic description of the general approach of his opponents:

Recall the old bad words we have for matter: matter is brute, inert, blind, senseless and purposeless. Mind on the other hand is light, subtle, discerning. Matter is stodgy; minds see visions and dream dreams. Matter is passive; minds create, act, and strive. Our entire religious tradition with its huge impact on how men see themselves has made the spiritual character of mind seem the plainest of truths. (1970, pp. 28–9)

2 Causes and choices

It has since the sixties become common to contrast 'agent causation' with 'event causation'. These labels are very misleading, and do in fact very frequently mislead. For they suggest that there is an important difference between *causing by* human actions and *causing by* those much more numerous events which are not human actions. That, however, is simply not the case. Suppose, for instance, that some action of mine – pressing a plunger, for example – causes something to occur – the blowing of a bridge, say – then this is causing in exactly the same sense as the similarly forceful impact of some accidentally falling object striking a similar detonator similarly connected. Both of these two causings – both the action, that is, and the event which is precisely not an action – make something happen. Both equally necessitate: both equally, that is to say, in consequence of their occurring in all the various circumstances given, make it (physically) inevitable that the same, actual explosive effect should occur and (physically) impossible that it should not.

(i) But the truth, by contrast, is that the crucial and relevant difference lies in the opposite direction. It is between the *being caused* to occur of human actions and the *being caused* to occur of all other events. In the modern literature the earliest entirely satisfactory account of this distinction is to be found in R. G. Collingwood's *An Essay on Metaphysics*. But few of those who have in recent years been writing about agent and event or – Heaven help us! – immanent and transeunt causation appear to have attended to either Plato or Collingwood (Flew and Vesey 1987). In that *Essay* Collingwood defines the first sense as that in which 'that which is "caused" is the free and deliberate action of a conscious and responsible agent, and "causing" him to do it means affording him a motive for doing it.' In the second sense, 'that which is "caused" is an event in nature, and its "cause" is an event or state of things by producing or preventing which we can produce or prevent that whose cause it is said to be' (1940, p. 285).

Illustrations of the employment of the word 'cause' and its logical associates in this second, wholly familiar sense would be superfluous. But, although its use in the first sense is in fact equally familiar, emphatic reminders are as essential as they have been rare. So consider, for example, my hearing of the news that some egregious enemy has suffered a misfortune. I may choose to construe this as a cause for celebration. If I do, then it will be correct both for me and for everybody else to say that my hearing of this news was both my reason for celebrating and the cause of my celebration. Nevertheless I was an agent in the whole business, not a patient. Nothing and no one forced me to celebrate, to make whoopee willy nilly. I could instead – and, had I been a nicer person, perhaps I would – have taken the acquisition of exactly the same information as a cause for commiseration. Had I chosen to respond in this way, it would then have been correct, both for me and for everyone else, to say that my hearing of this same news was both my reason for commiserating and/or the cause of my commiserating. So we have here a kind of case in which the very same cause may produce not merely a different but an opposite effect.

The differences just explained between two senses of 'cause' is so profound, and of such pervasive and fundamental importance, that it must be marked in a memorable way. As always the example to follow is that of the idiomatic distinction between 'funny' (ha ha) and 'funny' (peculiar). The problem is what to put in the brackets. In previous publications I proposed 'personal' and 'physical'. I now suggest that it is better to take a tip from Hume. In the essay 'Of National Characters' he writes: 'By *moral* causes, I mean all circumstances, which are fitted to work on the mind as motives or reasons...By *physical* causes I mean those qualities of the air and climate, which are supposed to work insensibly on the temper, by altering the tone and habit of the body...' (Hume [1742–77], p. 198). This specification assures us that moral causes are, in Plato's words, 'endowed with mind';

even if not, by the same token, always 'workers of things fair
and good'. But nothing in Hume's actual wording here requires
us to deny that physical causes necessitate; something which he,
of course, has to deny if his cherished 'reconciling project' is to
go through (Flew 1986a, ch. 8).

(ii) On another occasion we should need to go on much longer,
explicating the implications and applications of this fundamental
distinction between moral and physical causes. It would, for
instance, by illuminating to draw a parallel distinction between
moral and physical determinism; bringing out how wrong it is
to interpret the former – called by Freud 'psychic determinism'
– as a special case of, rather than as something incompatible with,
any necessitating physical determinism (Flew 1978, ch. 8). But
the point of including the present section 2 is, so far as possible,
to strengthen the case of those who would argue – in my view
quite mistakenly – that choosing creatures cannot be merely
material. So what has to come next is a demonstration, both that
we are indeed such choice creatures, and that our behaviour in
choosing and acting is not and could not have been physically
caused.

The question for us, therefore, is a question about choice. And
choice either is, or involves, or at any rate looks very like, what
in the *Treatise* Hume execrated as 'the liberty of *indifference*;
. . .which means a negation of necessity and causes' (Hume
[1739–40] II.iii.2, p. 407). If I am always causally necessitated
to behave in whatever turn out to be the ways in which I do in
fact behave, then it cannot also be the case, surely, that sometimes
I could, in some suitably strong sense, have behaved in some
fashion other than that in which I actually did behave? It is because
so many behavioural scientists believe, both that all human
behaviour is so caused, and that any psychological science must
presuppose that this is so, that they have to deny: both 'that
freedom exists' (Skinner 1948, ch. XXIX); and that anyone can
properly 'be held responsible for what he does, and justly punished
if he offends' (Skinner 1971, p. 19; compare Flew 1978, ch. 7).

But now, if this really is a necessary presupposition of any
psychological science, then it appears that there can be no such

science of human nature. For, in so far as we are indeed agents
– and to a greater or lesser extent throughout all our waking hours
we all are – we are, and cannot but be, making choices. This is
because it is always and necessarily true of all agents that they
could have done other than they did. Yet, if this is so, then we
cannot have been physically necessitated to act in whatever
particular fashion it was in which we did in fact (choose to)
act. In the most fundamental sense of 'able to do otherwise', the
ability or power to do otherwise is essentially involved in the
notions of agency or doing. If, in any of what Skinner would call
their behaviours, anyone could not in this most fundamental sense
– let us label it the 'agency' sense – have behaved in any other
way, then that behaviour cannot have been an action. It must have
been something which they observed, helplessly, rather than
something which they did, actively (Baier 1965).

This fundamental, 'agency' sense needs to be very firmly and
decisively distinguished from another – let us label that the
'acceptability' sense. For when we say that someone could not
have done otherwise (acceptability) we are not denying but, rather,
presupposing that in this case in fact he could (agency). Luther,
for instance, to reemploy a favourite illustration yet again, proclaimed famously to the Diet of Worms: 'Here I stand. I can no
other. So help me God.' But he was not, of course, in that
second sentence explaining that it was only a sudden general
paralysis which prevented him from scurrying off to some refuge
in Saxony.

Again, to reemploy another favourite illustration, when it is said
of some victim of criminal extortionists that he had had no choice,
that someone had made him an offer which he could not refuse,
this is not to be taken at the foot of the letter. It does not mean
that, quite literally, there was no choice between possible alternatives; that it was, therefore, not a case of agency at all. The point
in both cases, what is meant by saying that neither of these agents
could have acted other than they did, is that, although at least one
other option was in fact open to them, those actually chosen were
the only alternatives acceptable to them. We could not reasonably
have expected them to do otherwise, in either the prescriptive or
the descriptive sense of 'expect' (Flew 1975, 5.9 and 6.11).

(iii) Before proceeding to challenge the contention that these notions can properly be applied only to suppositious incorporeal entities, we must first do more, both to bring out what is logically involved in agency and choice, and to show that and how we can know, both that we do often act, and that in our actions we necessarily cannot be totally determined by physical necessities. A good place to start is the great chapter 'Of Power' in Locke's *Essay concerning Human Understanding*. Locke's prime concern is with personal power, as the ability at will to bring about this result instead of that, rather than with the powers of non-personal objects, which is a matter merely of what effects they will in fact produce if subjected to such and such conditions. There is a piquancy in taking this particular chapter (II.xxi) as our starting point for a journey in this direction. For Hume too used it in his own opposite attempts: attempts to show that we have no experience of physical necessity and physical impossibility; and that "The distinction, which we often make betwixt *power* and the exercise of it, is equally without foundation" (Hume [1739–40] I.iii.14, p. 171; and compare Flew 1986a, chs 5 and 8).

In trying to explain and to justify this idea of personal power Locke was handicapped by three Cartesian assumptions, all of which Hume also shared. The most important here, although it is not especially obtrusive in the two passages to be quoted, was the assumption that people are essentially incorporeal, controlling bodies which though not presently separate must be in principle separable. Thus Locke begins to explain what we have distinguished as personal power: 'This at least I think evident, That we find in our selves a *Power* to begin or forbear, continue or end several actions of our minds, and motions of our Bodies, barely by a thought or preference of the mind ordering, or as it were command the doing or not doing such or such a particular action. This *Power* is that which we call the *Will*' (II.xxi.5, p. 236).

The second passage is marred by the fact that Locke sees himself as spelling out what is meant by 'a free agent' rather than, more simply and more fundamentally, by 'an agent' or – and, surely, tautologically – 'a choosing agent'. The three Latin words refer to St Vitus's dance: 'Every one, I think, finds in himself a *Power* to begin or forbear. . . We have instances enough, and often more than enough in our own Bodies. A Man's Heart beats, and the Blood circulates, which 'tis not in his Power...to stop; and therefore in respect of these Motions, where rest depends not on his choice...he is not a *free Agent*. Convulsive Motions agitate his Legs, so that though he wills it never so much, he cannot ...stop their Motion, (as in that odd Disease called *chorea Sancti Viti*) but he is perpetually dancing. He is...under as much Necessity of moving, as a Stone that falls, or a Tennis-ball struck with a Racket. On the other side, a Palsie or the Stocks hinder his Legs...' (II.xxi.7 and 11, pp. 237 and 239).

In these two passages Locke at least suggested, even if it would perhaps be too generous to allow that he showed, that and how it must be possible to provide ostensive definitions of a whole connected cluster of key terms. To show how the argument will go, we have to insist on starting: not from such supposedly 'loose and separate' moments of consciousness as Lockean ideas or Humian 'perceptions of the mind'; but from bodily movements. Let those which can be either initiated or quashed at will be labelled 'movings', and those which cannot 'motions'. (These recommendations have the merit of going with rather than against the grain of common usage.)

Certainly it is obvious that there are plenty of marginal cases. Nevertheless, so long as there are, as there are, plenty – indeed far, far more – which fall unequivocally upon one side or the other, we must resolutely and stubbornly refuse to be prevented from insisting on a humanly vital distinction by any such diversionary appeals to the existence of marginal cases.

Now suppose that, for the moment, and for the sake of simplicity: we both ignore purely mental actions – such as summoning up a mental image; and refuse to make any distinction between those cases in which an agent chooses to move and those in which the choice is not to move. Then it becomes easy to recognize that the notions of action, of choice and of ability to do otherwise (agency) can be, and surely must be, explained by reference to what, given the previous simplifying assumptions, all actions must involve; namely, movings as distinct from motions. It also becomes, and this time without requiring any simplifying assumptions, easy to appreciate that all of us as agents are forever engaged in confronting ourselves with both physical necessities and their complementary physical impossibilities; and that by no means only or primarily in attempting to control some of our own bodily motions. (Here and always physical necessities and impossibilities are characterized as physical in implicit contrast with both logical and moral.)

Holding still to the same assumptions, it seems too that no one could ever be in a position consistently to assert, much less to know: either that there is no such thing as physically unnecessitated choice; or that there is no such thing as physical necessity. For it appears that chosen acts and physically necessitated occurrences are two opposites of such a kind that the nature of each can be explained only by pointing to actual specimens both of its own and of the other sort. Anyone, therefore, who is able to understand either of these two notions must have been acquainted with some specimens of both the two sorts of realities to which they respectively refer.

This is not a contention which it is either possible or necessary to establish here beyond all possibility of cavil. (But compare Flew and Vesey 1987, *passim*.) It will be sufficient simply to indicate that it does at least have considerable plausibility; and then to challenge doubters to falsify it, if they can, by developing ways of explaining these notions which do not involve and require such complementary ostension. Perhaps, after all, this is a trick which someone can turn. But until someone does, I shall myself continue to doubt the possibility. Though not from Missouri, I have to be shown!

(iv) One way of making the conclusions of the previous subsection more plausible is to indicate how it is that so many of the philosophical great and good have been misled to doubt, what now seems to me to be the manifest truth, that we are all of us constantly enjoying experience of both physical necessity and physically unnecessitated agency. Hume and so many others, surely, have been misled in large part because they have taken absolutely for granted three grossly false yet immensely seductive Cartesian presuppositions? One we have mentioned already, the assumption that people, or at any rate their minds or souls or selves, are essentially incorporeal. The other two also are both embedded, a little more deeply, in the explosively sensational second paragraph of Part IV of the *Discourse on the Method*. Cramming this pair into a single somewhat peremptory nutshell, these are: first, the assumption that all arguments must be either deductive or defective, since the only sufficient reasons for believing any proposition are (other) propositions which entail it; and, second, the notion that we are (all of us) forever imprisoned behind Veils of Appearance, since we can never be immediately aware of any mind-independent realities.

Given all this, then you are bound to start, as we insisted that we would not, with Lockean ideas or Humian 'perceptions of the mind' rather than with our two radically different kinds of bodily movement. I have already attempted elsewhere to show in some detail how these three Cartesian presuppositions misled Hume into error, both over this and in several other matters (Flew 1986a). So let us here consider instead the contention of one of our own contemporaries, who was taking issue with the 'kind of Incompatibilist that matters, the thinker who claims that we do have contra-causal free will...appealing to our ordinary belief, or knowledge, that an agent frequently *could have done otherwise* than he did' (Mackie 1982, pp. 166–7).

This author begins by complaining that it is difficult to say 'just what contra-causal free will would be', and then goes on to distinguish several interpretations of the key expression italicized above. Earlier subsections of the present section 2 have spelt out understandings both of agency as necessarily not physically necessitated and of the expression 'could have done otherwise' (agency); understandings which are, surely, satisfactorily strong? The counter-claim now is that 'contra-causal freedom, or the lack of it, simply is not the sort of thing of which we could have any "sense", any immediate introspective evidence' (1982, p. 168).

Maybe that is true. It is, nevertheless, entirely beside the point. For someone who refuses to accept those three Cartesian pre-suppositions will not be maintaining that which Hume undertakes to deny: 'It may be said, that we are every moment conscious of internal power; while we feel, that by the simple command of our will, we can move the organs of our body, or direct the faculties of our mind . . . This influence of the will we know by consciousness' (Hume [1748] VII.ii, p. 64). This may indeed be said, and often has been. But the new challenge does not start from an appeal to an allegedly familiar kind of logically private experience, but with an in principle public demonstration of the inexpugnable difference between two sorts of bodily movements: those which can be made or inhibited at will; and those which cannot. In this context, because the notions of physical necessity and physical impossibility have been ostensively defined by reference to that difference, stubbornly persistent claims that all such movements are by their sufficient physical causes equally necessitated become simply incoherent.

3 Inconceivables, or commonplaces?

The justification for devoting so much of the present chapter to 'Causes and choices' lies in the fact that agency, usually under the respectful description of Will, has been, along with rationality in every aspect, customarily epitomized with an equal respect as Reason, canonized as one of the two main and perhaps peculiarly human characteristics which many have considered not to be properly predicable of anything merely material. It was, therefore, necessary to display some of the connections between, on the one hand, Matter, and, on the other hand, Will and Reason. This now done, we can go on to notice that those accepting the suggestion that there is this kind of Great Divide may react in opposite ways: while some postulate immaterial subjects as the only possible bearers of such elevated predicates; others, believing that matter is all that there actually is, deny that such predicates can in fact have any correct application at all.

(i) The support of so many of the philosophical great and good notwithstanding, this suggestion that reason or will or personality cannot properly be predicated of anything merely material ought to be dismissed in the very shortest order. For it does not just happen to be mistaken. Nor is it an error to be uncovered only after long and painstaking inquiry. Instead it is the diametric opposite of a manifest and universally familiar truth. I will not resist the temptation to repeat a favourite piece of waspishness from the most acerbic of Classical scholars: 'Three minutes thought would suffice to find this out; but thought is irksome, and three minutes is a long time' (Housman 1931, p. xi).

The truth is that we have only one open question here: not whether these predicates can properly be attributed to anything corporeal; but whether they could properly be applied to anything else – whether, indeed, there could be anything else to which they could significantly be applied. For our paradigm cases for learning and teaching the meanings of all the relevant words and expressions all are, and could scarcely fail to be, cases of their applications to those themselves paradigmatically corporeal creatures, people. What else do we know to which they could or can be applied, unequivocally and without semantic shifts?

That a suggestion so contrary to common sense and common experience should to so many seem to inescapably sound is a phenomenon crying out for explanation. Presumably a large part of that explanation must lie in the fact that most of the people concerned have been clients of theories or definitions which arbitrarily attribute to matter characteristics forbidding any admission that creatures constituted of nothing else but such stuff as this could possess the powers of persons. Berkeley, for instance, is sometimes almost petulant in his abuse of matter: it is not just 'unthinking'; but it is also – which is scarcely consistent – 'stupid'.

Another part of the explanation perhaps lies in the temptation to accept what are felt to be compelling abstract principles as self-evidently true, despite their contrariety to unavoidable concrete experience. For instance: among the 'Axioms or Common Principles' in the addendum to the second set of objections to the *Meditations* Descartes offers as the fourth: 'Whatever reality or perfection exists in a thing, exists formally or else eminently in its first and total cause.' Yet, seemingly, this denies the wholly familiar fact that trivial causes often produce most important effects. Again, innumerable people have considered it to be luminously obvious that creatures so complicated and so well adapted as living organisms could not but be products of some sort of design and manufacture. Yet Topsy – never exposed to any sophisticated miseducation – was surely right to insist that all available direct evidence strongly supported her own claim: 'They just growed.' Had Topsy had the advantage of acquaintance with the works of C. D. Broad she might have coined a truly Broadian label for all such pieces of supposedly self-evident endarkenment: 'Counter-evidential Empirical Intuitions'.

(ii) The alternative reaction is to argue that, since nothing purely material can possess such characteristics, and since even the human organism is purely material, we must conclude that it is wrong to attribute them to people. This is done most obviously and most regularly by certain scientists and still more by certain philosophers who see themselves as political (or philosophical) commissars for science: who believe that it has been revealed to them – perhaps first by Leucippus or Democritus or perhaps later by hypostatized Science – that all changes in and movements of matter are subject always to total and absolute physical necessitations; and who from this revelation infer that they have to deny the reality of agency and choice; or, as they would say, of free will. About this I will say here only one thing. That it is curious that many of those most eager to tell the world that the rise of Quantum Mechanics was the death knell of Laplacian determinism are at the same time most stubborn in their refusal to allow that the most complicated systems in the known Universe may be to some extent exempt from such total physical necessitation. (But compare Flew and Vesey 1987, *passim*.)

Chapter Five
Aristotle and Aquinas

...mind naked and simple, apart from any organ of
perception, seems to elude the conceptual powers of our
understanding.

M. T. Cicero, *de natura deorum* (*On the Nature of the Gods*)
(1967), I (xi)

But to what purpose, may some man say, is such subtlety in
a work of this nature...? It is to this purpose, that men may
no longer suffer themselves to be abused, by them, that by
this doctrine of *separated essences*, built on the vain
philosophy of Aristotle, would fright them...as men fright
birds from the corn with an empty doublet, a hat, and a
crooked stick. For it is upon this ground, that when a man is
dead and buried, they say his soul, that is his life, can walk
separated from his body...Upon the same ground they say,
that the figure, and colour, and taste of a piece of bread, has
a being there, where they say there is no bread.

Thomas Hobbes, *Leviathan* (1961), IV (xlvi), vol. IV, pp. 674–5

The question of the ontologically dualistic or monistic nature of
man is one of the several in which it can prove profitable to contrast traditions stemming from Plato with traditions inspired by
Aristotle. Yet here, as in most other cases, there are at least some
suggestions in Aristotle of what his admirers will be inclined to
regret as Platonic hangups. It was upon these suggestions in 'the
vain philosophy of Aristotle' that St Thomas Aquinas built in
developing his doctrine that a separable, separated, surviving form

or essence of a person would maintain the identity of that person between death and resurrection, thus overcoming the Replica Objection.

1 Aristotle, and the immortality of the intellect

Remembering all that was said in chapter three about the etymological connections between various key terms, Aristotle's treatise *de anima* [On the Soul] should in the first instance be seen as a philosophical study of life. Its declared aim is 'to contemplate and to know its nature and essence' (402A7–8). This means, or should mean, that he will be using the word 'soul' in the sense in which to talk about something having a soul is simply a misleadingly substantival way of saying that it is alive. Consequently, when Aristotle speaks of the vegetative, or the sensitive, or the rational soul, what he is discussing is the capacities to grow, decay, feed, and reproduce; the capacities to see and to desire; and the capacity to think, respectively. It is perhaps not altogether surprising that even he seems sometimes to have been entangled by this terminology.

At times he takes it that the dividing lines between the levels in this hierarchy of functions must be more absolute than they are. At other times he even appears to forget that, in this understanding of the word 'soul', souls cannot be substances (in our sense, that is; a sense quite different from that in which Aristotle himself employs the Greek word usually translated 'substance'). His starting point is the soul as the principle of life; and, although he does not make our distinction between criterial and causal interpretations of this expression, his present methods and concerns certainly are directed more to the former than to the latter. In so far as that is so, however, to offer 'The soul' as your answer to the questions 'What makes living things alive?' or 'In virtue of what are living things called alive?' is something less than excitingly informative. It is much too like offering 'Their contents' as an answer to the question 'What did the pockets contain?' It must, however, also be emphasized that when Aristotle talks about the essence of something he is to be interpreted as thinking of its true or proper, and by no means arbitrary, definition: the discovery of such an essence is to be rated a revelation of reality rather than an exercise in lexicography. So, while we may be disappointed, we should not be surprised to discover that Aristotle goes on almost immediately to entertain the notion that souls might be separable; and therefore, in our sense, substantial.

(i) Thus, only half-way through his very first chapter, he writes: 'There is a further difficulty about the predicates of the soul. Are they all shared by that of which it is the soul, or is there something peculiar to the soul alone? We have got to deal with this. But it is not easy' (403A3–5). The reason why this matters is, he contends, that 'if any of the functions and affections of the soul are peculiar to it, it will be possible for the soul to be separated. If, on the other hand, there is nothing peculiar to it, then it will not be capable of separate existence' (403A10–12). By the end of the chapter Aristotle has recovered himself. The seed of suggestion has, however, been planted.

His most characteristic and fundamental thesis is that the individual life or soul is the form, or the essence, or the what-it-is-to-be (the 'quiddity') of the particular organism. This Aristotelian notion of form or essence or quiddity – that last a barbarous term derived from Scholastic Latin – is tricky, and must be distinguished with especial care from that of Plato's Forms or Ideas. R. D. Hicks, the editor of what was for many years the standard English language edition of *de anima* tells us that by this thesis Aristotle 'so far from favouring materialism, secures once and for all the soul's absolute immateriality' (p. xliii).

In a sense this is true. Aristotle does indeed most categorically reject all ideas of the soul as some sort of lump of stuff. But it could also be most misleading. For his basic contention is utterly un-Platonic, and leaves no room at all for any doctrine of immortality. Certainly, an Aristotelian form is no more a corporeal thing than a Platonic Form would be. But then it is not an incorporeal one either. It is not, in the crucial sense, a substance at all. The soul as the form stands to the stuff of the particular body as the configuration of the statue to the materials of which it is made, as vision to the eye capable of seeing, as cutting power to the serviceable axe (the illustrations are all Aristotle's). Whatever else may be obscure here, it is, as Aristotle himself said, obvious that the soul is not separable from the body. And, furthermore, this inseparability must be a matter not of physical but of logical impossibility. It is upon this insistence that we must rest Aristotle's claim to be regarded as the patron of all monistic and materialistic views of the nature of man.

Had this been all that Aristotle said, the whole picture would have been conveniently sharp, neat, and clear. Unfortunately, as we began to see before, he also had what look like Platonic reservations. These have been, historically, very important. They apply to the intellectual aspects of man, and to the corresponding intellectual (functions of the) soul. Unfortunately again, despite the enormous labours of the commentators, it still remains very far from certain precisely what Aristotle did think here, or why; possibly because he himself had not in fact formed any firm and precise opinion. Nevertheless some relevant points can usefully be put.

(ii) First: suppose we follow the tradition, descending from Alexander of Aphrodisias through Averrhoes ('The Commentator'), which attributes to Aristotle a belief in some sort of Eternal Intellect. Then it is clear that this is still not a doctrine of personal immortality, offering to the likes of St Augustine a gratifying prospect of future rewards (for themselves) and promised punishments (for others) – a point emphasized, with unwonted heat, by St. Thomas Aquinas in his polemical pamphlet *de unitate intellectus contra Averrhoistas Parisienses* [On the Unity of the Intellect against the Parisian Averrhoists]. Furthermore, since this Abstract Intellect, as opposed to the intellects of particular men, must be necessarily unique, it is not at all the right material to serve Aquinas's own vital theoretical need for bridges between us as individuals and our postulated individual successors.

Second: the one kind of reason which might be proffered for saying that the Abstract Intellect (or, for that matter, any other putative Abstract Reality) is essentially eternal is, really, no sort of reason for saying that anything at all in fact goes on for ever. It is, in a way, correct to say that such things as necessary truths and the logical relations between concepts are somehow timeless and eternal. Yet this is certainly not a matter of anything imperishable actually existing, but rather of its just not making sense to ask temporal questions about the periods during which these truths and these relations obtain. From eternity, in this sense, we can have nothing either to hope or to fear.

Third: supposing that Aristotle really had wanted to suggest that individual intellects could and would survive, then, presumably, a large part of his reason would have lain in his belief that ratiocination, unlike sight or hearing, is not localized in any organ. Even if this belief had not turned out to be erroneous, it would still have been necessary to insist that the absence of any specialist (corporeal) organ provides no justification for assuming that our intellectual attributes must, or even might, be those of incorporeal substances. The lack of specialist organs of melancholy or of volition is surely not to be construed as providing grounds for seeking invisible subjects to which to attribute Eric's feeling glum or Katrina's wanting to go to sleep. These and other more intellectual characteristics are, simply and obviously, attributes of the people concerned. Aristotle himself never employed any such easily disposable argument. What he argued here was that the intellect, 'since it thinks all things, must needs [in the words of Anaxagoras] be unmixed with any, if it is to rule, that is, to know' (429A18–29).

This dark saying has been construed as an expression of a belief that our intellects are both incorporeal and substances: a belief which might seem to mesh in well with Aristotle's undoubted conviction that abstract cognition is something rather grand, divine even – just the job for the top sort of person. Certainly, as he makes very clear in the *Nicomachean Ethics* (X.vii), he did believe that both the highest style of life and the happiest is the life of the intellect; and that anyone who attains this attains it 'in virtue of something within him that is divine' (1177B29). But the cherishing of an ideal of this kind is, as we saw in section 4 (iii) of chapter three, entirely consistent with a rejection of any notion of personal immortality.

(iii) The nearest Aristotle comes to deploying a formal argument in support of his doctrine, whatever it may be, is in chapter 4 of Book I. He begins: 'Doubtless it would be better not to say that the soul pities or learns or thinks, but that the man does so with the soul: and this too, not in the sense that the motion occurs in the soul, but in the sense that motion sometimes reaches to, sometimes starts from, the soul' (408B13–16).

That was not a good start. Certainly it would be better not to say that either the mind or the soul either pities or learns or thinks, or indeed that it does anything else. But the preferable alternative is to say that it is the person who pities or learns or thinks or what have you. For if you insist on saying that either the man or the woman – or even the sexually indeterminate person – does this or that with their soul then you may be tempted – especially in the context of a treatise on the soul – to construe your idiom in an instrumental rather than an adverbial way. Yet to read any Greek analogues of such phrases as 'with my whole mind' as referring to the instrumentality of some personal portion of not-matter, instead of to the manner in which some activity was performed, would be as grossly, as grotesquely wrong as to look for a dog's lost temper or the grin finally detached from the grinning face.

Aristotle proceeds:

But intellect would seem to be developed in us as a self-existing substance and to be imperishable. For, if anything could destroy it, it would be the feebleness of age. But, as things are, no doubt what occurs is the same as with the sense organs. If an aged man could procure an eye of the right sort, he would see just as well as a young man. Hence old age must be due to an affection or state not of the soul as such, but of that in which the soul resides, just as is the case in intoxication and disease. In like manner, then, though and the exercise of knowledge are enfeebled through the loss of something else within, but are themselves impassive. (408B19–25)

'This', as Wittgenstein so often said, 'is a terrible argument; just terrible.' Of course old age, like intoxication and disease, afflicts some but only creatures of flesh and blood – specifically old people, drunks and sick people. And maybe if the transplant surgeons could give me two young eyes I could see much better than I do now. Maybe too if the brains of the senile demented could be replaced with younger, well stocked substitutes they would think better. But, even granting all this, it simply does not begin to look like showing that intellect is 'developed in us as a self-existing substance', which is 'impassive' and hence 'imperishable'.

Aristotle continues:

> But reasoning, love and hatred are not attributes of the thinking faculty but of its individual possessor, in so far as he possesses it. Hence when this possessor perishes there is neither memory nor love: for these never did belong to the thinking faculty, but to the composite whole which has perished; while the intellect – doubtless a thing more divine – is impassive. (408B25–9)

Well, maybe it is a thing more divine. But that is no reason why intellect and the faculty of thinking cannot be, like love and hatred, and as they are, attributes of their individual possessors; in so far as they do possess them. We have still been given no reason why we should allow mind or intellect to be separable, and a substance.

On the contrary: Aristotle has elsewhere insisted that 'intellect has no other nature than this, that it is a capacity' (429A21–2). But a capacity, surely, is not at all the sort of thing which could significantly be said to exist separately? A faculty or a capacity, unlike the person who is endowed with this faculty or capacity, could not exist independently of anyone or anything so endowed. Sometimes one suspects even Aristotle of occasionally slipping into the false assumption – so regularly and so rightly belaboured by Berkeley – that every substantive is a word for a sort of substances. Nor, we must add, is it only love and memory and hatred which 'never did belong to the thinking faculty'. That faculty – like all the various desires, dispositions, and all the other faculties which a person may have – itself belongs to, in as much as it is and can only be an attribute of, the person.

(iv) All in all the correct conclusion seems to be that Aristotle's treatment of the possible separability and consequent immortality of the intellect was an aberration. Certainly any attempt to recruit these tentative probings as support for 'the logically unique expectation' has to be stopped short by noticing the abrupt contempt with which he elsewhere inhibits any such immortal longings. Thus we are told in the *Nicomachean Ethics*: 'Choice cannot have for its object impossibilities: if a man were to say he chose something impossible he would be thought a fool; but we can wish for things that are impossible, for instance immortality' (1111B21–4).

Nor should we overlook the fact that in the whole range of Aristotle's works there is no positive treatment of the question of a future life, nor yet even any promise of such treatment. There was during the late fifteenth and early sixteenth centuries in the universities much discussion both of the interpretation of Aristotle and of the substantive issue of the nature of the soul. It is said that in those days – days remarkably different from ours! – students often interrupted lectures with impatient cries of 'Quid de anima?' (Douglas 1910, ch. 4). In the long and frequently furious controversy of that period the effective last word was said by Pietro Pomponazzi – the Peter of Mantua often hailed as 'the last of the Schoolmen and the first of the Aristotelians'. Book IX of his great polemic *de immortalitate animae* [On the Immortality of the Soul] concluded: first, on his own account and on the substantive issue, that the soul, including the intellect, 'is in no way truly itself an individual. And so it is truly a form beginning with and ceasing to be with the body'; and then, second, and on the issue of interpretation, that any other view is totally un-Aristotelian.

2 The expedients of Aquinas

Whatever the truth about the correct interpretation of Aristotle, it certainly is the case that it was passages such as those discussed in the previous section 1 which gave Aquinas purchase for developing, within a generally Aristotelian framework of categories, an incongruously Platonic notion. Aquinas had, as we saw in section 2 of chapter one, the most urgent theoretical reasons for wanting to maintain that the soul is, after all, a substance; or, as he himself puts it, a subsistent thing. Above all he wanted to reconcile two apparently incompatible inclinations of his own teacher, Albertus Magnus: 'When I consider the soul in itself, I agree with Plato; but, when I consider it with respect to the form of life which it gives to its body, I agree with Aristotle' (quoted in Robb 1984, p. 19). With this 'reconciling project' in mind Aquinas was bound to recognize as both a hint and a challenge one of the sentences already quoted from Aristotle's *de anima*: '...if any of the functions of the soul are peculiar to it, it will be possible for the soul to be separated' (403A10–12).

(i) In his *Commentary* upon that work Aquinas argues, with reference to a passage quoted in the previous section 1(iii):

But our intellect...must itself lack all those things which its nature understands. Since then it naturally understands all sensible and bodily things, it must be lacking in every bodily nature; just as the sense of sight, being able to know colour, lacks all colour. If sight itself had any particular colour, this colour would prevent it from seeing other colours, just as the tongue of a feverish man, being coated with a bitter moisture, cannot taste anything sweet.

If this is indeed what Aristotle meant, then his position was indefensible. For if intellect is, reasonably enough, to be compared with the sense of sight, it is because they are both (cognitive) capacities. But we need no particular argument to show why a capacity, as opposed to the subject possessing that capacity, cannot itself have any material characteristics. The reason why the sense of sight is not yellow is: not that being yellow must render it (or its possessor) incapable of seeing yellow things, in particular; but that, quite generally, it would be nonsense to attribute this or any other sensible characteristic to any capacity at all. (It would also seem to follow from Aristotle's principle, as expounded by Aquinas, that intellect cannot understand intellect.)

It might seem that it is upon precisely this lamentable argument that in the *Summa theologica* Aquinas himself relies, to establish what is for him the absolutely vital conclusion: 'that the principle of intellectual operation which we call the soul is...both incorporeal and subsistent'. For he even employs there the same example of 'a sick man's tongue'. However, his comparison is between the soul (as 'the principle of intellectual operation') and the *organ* of sight (not the *sense*).

Answering the question 'Whether the soul is a body?' he first identifies soul with life: 'To seek the nature of the soul, we must premise that the soul is defined as the first principle of life in those things which live: for we call living things *animate*, and those which are not alive *inanimate*.' But he then brings in knowledge, which, surely cannot in any understanding be accepted as characteristic of all life: 'Now life is shown principally by two actions, knowledge and motion.' His chief concern here is to reject what we have distinguished as a causal construction, as opposed to a criterial, of the expression 'principle of life'. To prove his conclusion he appeals to what he calls 'universal and certain principles'. But these will not have the same felt force for those unschooled in Aristotelian technicalities. That conclusion is: 'The philosophers of old, not being able to rise above their imagination, supposed that the principle of these actions was something corporeal. For they asserted that only bodies were real things, and that what is not corporeal is nothing' (I.lxxv.A1).

The question addressed by the immediately subsequent Article 2 is 'Whether the soul is a subsistent thing?' Aquinas, as usual, conscientiously confronts himself with what he sees as the strongest possible opposition. The first objection which he considers here is that substances, in his and our sense of 'substances', are particulars: 'But it is not the soul which is *this particular thing* but the composite of soul and body.' The second is that substances can be said to operate. 'But the soul does not operate; for, as it says in *de anima* Book I, "to say that the soul feels or understands is like saying that it weaves or builds".' Finally, Objection 3 is that, if the soul were a substance, it would have some operation apart from the body. 'But it has no operation apart from the body, not even understanding. For understanding does not occur without a phantasm, nor a phantasm without a body.'

The word 'phantasm' is equivalent to the expression 'mental image'. That imageless thought is impossible is a very ancient conviction, dating back far earlier than the thirteenth century. So Aquinas can go on at once to quote from St Augustine's *de*

Trinitate [On the Trinity] to provide the kernel of his own answer to that last objection: ' ''Whoever appreciates that the nature of the soul is to be a substance and not corporeal will see that those who believe that it is corporeal are led astray through incorporating into it those things without which they are unable to think of any nature – namely, mental images of material things''.'

No doubt this is what, were it once granted 'that the nature of the soul is to be a substance and not corporeal', it would be reasonable to say. By the way: those still living in the intellectual world which Descartes made should all take note that, before that Cartesian turn, it used to appear altogether obvious to everyone that not only mental images of physical objects but also sense-data belonged to the sphere, not of mind or soul, but of matter. Aquinas, however, offers in support of St Augustine's premise, argument which is bound to strike any present day student as factitious and feeble.

In the main body of this key article, after restating what he has undertaken to prove, Aquinas writes:

Now it is obvious that man can through his intellect have knowledge of the natures of all material things. But what can have knowledge of a certain kind of objects cannot have anything of those objects in its own nature; because that which was in it naturally would get in the way of its knowing any other objects of the same sort. Thus we observe that a sick man's tongue, vitiated by a feverish and bitter humour, cannot taste anything sweet; but to it everything seems bitter. If, therefore, the intellectual principle contained in itself the nature of any body it could not know all bodies. Now every body has its own determinate nature. Therefore it is impossible for the intellectual principle to be a body. It is likewise impossible for it to understand by means of bodily organ, since the particular nature of the organ would prevent its knowing all bodies. Compare the way in which liquid put into a glass vase seems to be of the same colour, not only when some particular colour is in the pupil of the eye but even when it is in the vase. (I.lxxv.A2)

Once this argument has been thus fully and confidently deployed, anyone not crushed by the weight of Thomas's own and, vicariously, of his Church's authority will want to put two sharp, sceptical questions to the Angelic Doctor: 'How are we supposed to be able to know: that "what can have knowledge of a certain kind of objects cannot have anything of those objects in its own nature"; and that "that which was in it naturally would get in the way of its knowing any other objects of the same sort"?'

Suppose that we start by working with the Saint's own example of the eye as the organ of sight. Eyes are material. Yet that certainly does not prevent us from using them for seeing (and, if you must, knowing) material things, including other people's eyes and even – in mirrors – our own. Furthermore, even if this Thomist principle did fit all the facts about our present sense organs, this would at most suggest that it was a contingent truth about these. To serve his purpose it must he known to be, if not actually necessary, at least sufficiently universal to apply not only to sense organs but also to 'that principle of intellectual operation which we call the soul' – something which he himself is concerned to show to be radically different. If once we have become aware of the existence of that cognitive underclass, then the foundation principle of this entire attempt at demonstration is exposed as one more example of what was earlier, and rather mischievously, dubbed a 'Counter-evidential Empirical Intuition'.

(ii) In later articles falling within the same Question of the *Summa theologica* St Thomas Aquinas proceeds to argue: that the souls of tbe brutes – animals other than man – are not similarly subsistent things (A3); that human souls are naturally incorruptible (A6); and that, although – as we saw in chapter one – the human soul is supposed to provide sufficient continuity between death and resurrection to maintain personal identity, the individual human soul is most emphatically not the whole individual person (A4). But, since the support for the first step in this progress was so wretched, we have to ask whether anyone else could develop a better alternative. It is unfortunate that no such attempt appears to have been made by any of those of our contemporaries combining lively philosophical sophistication with commitment to the same faith as St Thomas.

The nearest approach known to me is in Peter Geach's *God and the Soul*. Repudiating as 'a savage superstition' any Platonic–Cartesian view, he adds that 'the superstition is not mended but rather aggravated by conceptual confusion, if the soul-piece is supposed to be immaterial . . . The only tenable conception of the soul is the Aristotelian conception as the form, or actual organization, of the living body . . .' (Geach 1969, p. 38). Yet the only mention of Aquinas in the present context is to notice that he was convined that there are disembodied spirits 'but ones that cannot see or hear or feel pain or fear or anger; he allowed them no mental operations except those of thought and will. Damned spirits would suffer from frustration of their evil will, but not from aches and pains or foul odours or the like' (1969, p. 22).

Geach makes it manifest that he himself has grave doubts whether this particular conviction of St Thomas can be sustained. One reason, surely, which Geach had no occasion to give, is that will cannot be thus totally detached from desire, while desire is an attribute exclusively of living things. The point is well put in *de corpore* [On Body] by a philosopher whom we both, I believe, admire: ' . . . the same thing is called both will and appetite; but the consideration of them, namely, before and after deliberation, is divers. Nor is that which is done within a man whilst he willeth anything, different from that which is done in other living creatures, whilst deliberation having preceded, they have appetite' (Hobbes IV.xxv.25, I. p. 409).

The only hope for a separated soul, therefore, lies in thinking rather than willing: it was prudent of St Thomas to summon knowledge in addition to motion as a second essential characteristic of life or soul! But Geach himself is ambivalent about the separability of thinking. After first asserting that 'in our present experience we encounter thought as an activity of organisms' (1969, p. 38), he goes on to suggest that 'since thought is in principle not locatable in the physical time continuum' (p. 38) it is conceivable that thoughts 'originated by no living organism' (p. 39) might be 'embodied in the numbers spelt out by' (p. 39) a roulette wheel. Nevertheless on the next two pages Geach appears to take it all back, again asserting that thinking is 'a vital activity, which can only be performed by a living being' (p. 40). He adds two characteristically fierce comments: 'the arguments used to the contrary are often frivolously bad' (p. 40); and 'such arguments give an impression of willing self-deception' (p. 41).

Geach is here, surely, confusing two quite different contentions about thought? Both are both true and important. But neither possesses sufficient strength to sustain a thesis of substantial separability. Nor, even if it were, would any such separated substance be enough of a particular individual to constitute the tie of personal identity between one person, long since definitely dead, and the best of replicas, now supposedly resurrected.

The first of these true and important contentions is that the logical aspects of thoughts are timeless. Yet this can scarcely be accounted a relevant reason for suggesting that active thinking might conceivably be embodied in the numbers spelt out successively by an autonomously spinning roulette wheel. The second and equally sound contention is that the same thoughts may be expressed in many different ways: the software is separable from the hardware; and the same programs could, at least in principle, be developed to be run through either an electronic or a mechanical computer.

Certainly these are truths about thoughts which have led many to suggest that thinking must involve an element somehow supernatural and outwith the scope of materialistic science. For instance: the contention that scientific naturalism is self-refuting, because – allegedly – it leaves no room for our having and giving adequate evidencing reasons for our beliefs, was a main item in the apologetic stock in trade of C. S. Lewis: an item displayed most exhaustively in his best-selling book *Miracles: A Preliminary Study* (1960). In its crudest form this contention was during the late forties brilliantly demolished by 'A Reply to Mr C. S. Lewis's Argument that "Naturalism" is Self-refuting', a paper only very recently accorded more than a lamentably local and limited publication (Anscombe 1981, II, pp. 224–32).

In the context of our insistence upon an unreservedly Aristotelian approach to all questions about the nature of man there are two further points to make. In the first place, the fundamental distinctions between three categorically different inquiries about the sayings and doings of people need to be presented, exactly as they are, as inquiries about the sayings and doings of creatures of flesh and blood: every step up the ladder of abstraction constitutes a dangerous move towards detachment from concrete realities.

So let us consider a specimen of a behaviour to which we should normally react, and which we should normally describe, as the making of an assertion. And let us select as the proposition asserted not boring old p but 'The death of Jan Masaryk was not suicide but murder.' Now two totally different interpretations may be put on the question, 'Why did she make that assertion?' In one it is construed as asking for her evidencing reasons for believing that the proposition in question is true. Here any discussion ought sooner rather than later to refer to Claire Sterling's definitive study, *The Masaryk Case* (1982). In the other interpretation the questioner wants to learn the agent's motivating reason for making this assertion on this particular occasion; and is not concerned, or is not immediately concerned, with either the truth of the proposition or the evidence available to its assertor. The categorically right kind of answer in this second case would be: 'In order to provoke and flush out some of those insincerely claiming to have repudiated everything embraced under the deliberately indefinite description "Stalinism".' One excellent way of enforcing this most important distinction between evidencing and motivating reasons is by reference to the Wager Argument of Pascal. For that is unique among the traditional arguments for belief in God in its abandonment of the search for the former in favour of urging the latter (Flew 197 1, pp. 218-2 1; and compare Flew 1982).

It should be obvious that reasons of these two sorts are not competitors for the same logical space: it is perfectly possible to have, at one and the same time, both sufficient evidencing reasons to warrant a claim to know some proposition, and adequate motivating reasons to justify your action of asserting that proposition (Flew 1978, ch. 5). But it is far less clear that there is no incompatibility between either of these two and possible physical causes of that behaviour. For there is a third way in which we conceivably could, yet very rarely would, react to and describe what we should normally react to and describe as the making of an assertion. We could, that is to say, refuse to interpret the sounds proceeding from the assertor's mouth as a meaningful utterance, but instead consider it solely in its aspect as so much physiologically produced acoustic disturbances. In that perspective the explanatory questions unambiguously demand answers in terms of physical causation.

This brings us to the second further point. For, as was argued in chapter four, the behaviour involved in acting for motivating reasons cannot be completely necessitated by physical causes. So, if all the movements of all matter were always the outcome of such physical necessitations, and so long as we continue to recognize the reality of action, with its permanent possibility of doing otherwise, then it might seem that there would be no alternative to allowing that some immaterial and thus presumably supernatural agent is at work in and on the human organism – necessitating those movements of and in that organism which without such supernatural intervention would not have taken the form and direction which in fact they did take. The second further point is to note that all this has a bearing upon not only our practical but also our theoretical reason.

This is something to which Sir Karl Popper has recently given prominence. In *The Open Universe: An Argument for Indeterminism* he restored and vastly improved an old argument. In the late fifties various much inferior but then more fashionable versions were subjected to effectively destructive criticism (Flew 1958 and 1959). Popper's revised version, which he credits to Descartes, introduces choice as its key idea: 'The point... is... that *a critical grasp of truth*, and a proper assessment of an argument, must be a free, voluntary action of ours (rather than the reaction of a recording machine)...' (Popper 1982, p. 81). But Popper is not prepared to claim that 'this somewhat strange argument' refutes 'the doctrine of "scientific" determinism. Even if it is accepted as valid, the world may still be as described by "scientific" determinism' (1982, p. 85).

The reason why Popper refuses to make the bolder claim, to know that universal physical determinism is false, is the same as the reason why he feels that he has to maintain some other, notoriously paradoxical positions. It is that he, like our mutual philosophical hero Hume, has never brought himself radically to review and reject the three ruinous presuppositions revealed in the second paragraph of Part IV of the *Discourse on the Method* (Flew 1986a). The particular presuppositions obstructing Popper's view in the present case are that people are essentially incorporeal and that we can be immediately aware only of our own Humian 'ideas and impressions'. How else indeed are we to explain: either Popper's inability to see that we all have abundant experience of being able to do otherwise; or his assumption that an appeal to this experience is an appeal to some such Humian 'perception of the mind'? It is sadly significant that in the first two sentences of his book he announces: 'I intend to set forth here my reasons for being an indeterminist. I shall not include among these reasons the intuitive idea of free will: as a rational argument in favour of indeterminism it is useless' (Popper 1982, p. 1). Nevertheless, as we have shown, it is not.

Chapter Six
The Cartesian Turn

Descartes, dans l'histoire de la pensée, ce sera toujours le
cavalier français qui partit d'un si bon pas.

> Charles Péguy, *Note conjointe sur M. Descartes
> et la philosophie cartésienne* (1957), p. 1303

Nous disons les choses en français comme l'esprit est forcé
de les considérer en quelque langue qu'on écrive. Ciceron a
pour ainsi dire suivi la syntaxe française avant que d'obéir à
la syntaxe latine.

> Denis Diderot, *Lettre sur les sourds et muets à l'usage
> de ceux qui entendent et qui parlent* (1978), IV, p. 164

Just as Goethe, who was present, said that the cannonade of Valmy
opened a new era in human history, so, with equal truth, it can
be asserted that the modern period in philosophy starts with this
single devastating sentence:

Thus, because our senses sometimes play us false, I decided to suppose
that there was nothing at all which was such as they cause us to imagine
it; and, because there are men who make mistakes in reasoning even
in the simplest geometrical matters, and construct specious sophisms,
I, judging that I was as liable to error as anyone else, rejected as unsound
all those reasonings which I had hitherto accepted as demonstrations.
(Descartes 1934, I, p. 101)

Many objections have, of course, been deployed against what
is thus presented as a programme for doubting systematically
everything which conceivably could be doubted. C. S. Peirce,

for instance, urged that all our individual inquiries have to start from wherever we individually happen to be: 'We cannot begin with complete doubt. We must begin with all the prejudices which we actually have. . .Those prejudices are not to be dispelled by a maxim. . .' Peirce, however, proceeds in the same paragraph to a cautious concession: 'A person may, it is true, find reason to doubt what he began by believing; but in that case he doubts because he has a positive reason for it, and not on account of the Cartesian maxim' (Peirce 1931–5, V, pp. 156–7).

Peirce's charge is nowadays usually brought in a more conceptual-analytic form: all doubt presupposes some knowledge, or at least some belief sufficiently plausible to constitute a reason. It would, that is to say, be a solecism to profess to be doubting, as opposed to confessing plain nescience concerning, any proposition in an area in which one was totally ignorant. To which it might well be added that a 'doubt' which is shielded against all the demands of action, as were all the 'doubts' in that (room with a) stove, in which Descartes is supposed to have accomplished his intellectual revolution, is not a genuine doubt; any more than a 'belief' which carries no implications for actual or possible behaviour is a genuine belief.

But Descartes has a complete answer to the main charge here, albeit an answer which is for him correspondingly catastrophic. He has offered reasons for doubting: both the truth of all his previous beliefs about the Universe around him; and the validity of all his previous reasonings. The trouble is that these retail reasons are flat inconsistent with the wholesale proposals they are supposed to support. It really will not do to argue – as, surely, Descartes is arguing? – that all my beliefs (in some very wide area) have been only doubtfully true, and that all my reasonings (perhaps on every subject) have been only doubtfully sound, *on the grounds that* some of my earlier beliefs about the truth of falsity of such propositions, and some of my earlier judgements about the validity or invalidity of arguments, later turned out, and are now presumably known, to have been mistaken.

There is also a further inconsistency, still more fundamental. These Cartesian 'doubts' cannot be formulated or understood without assuming some knowledge of kinds which Descartes is setting himself to repudiate. For how could we allow that anyone was master of the concepts of material thing and of hallucination, of valid and of invalid argument, of dreaming and of waking, if they were unable confidently and correctly to identify any specimen exemplars, however paradigmatic? Descartes is taking for granted his own mastery of colloquial French; and in the somewhat later *Meditations*, of Latin also. Yet this is knowledge of a kind and amount which we could not concede to be possessed by anyone pretending to such near total Cartesian uncertainty (Flew 1971, chs VII, 1–4, and VIII).

For us, however, what is most instructive is the failure to apply the programme of systematic doubt to beliefs of precisely that kind to which Descartes himself had earlier been arguing that it must be most applicable. Thus in Part I of the *Discourse*, while reviewing his own education, Descartes contrasts philosophy with theology, rather sharply: '. . . theology teaches how to gain Heaven; . . . philosophy gives the means by which one can speak plausibly on all matters and win the admiration of the less learned . . .' He then affirms his own commitment: 'I revered our theology, and aspired as much as anyone else to gain Heaven; but . . . the revealed truths which lead to it are beyond our understanding . . . to undertake the examination of them, and succeed, one would need some special grace from Heaven, and to be more than a man' (1934, I, p. 85).

Considered by itself this may be all very well. Yet what it certainly does not do is consist with one very pertinent remark made later in the same Part I. This is a remark which it would be salutary to apply also, with equal sharpness, to the speculations of Descartes himself in (the room with) the stove:

For it seemed to me that I might find much more truth in the reasonings which someone makes in matters that affect him closely, the results of which must be detrimental to him if his judgement is faulty, than from the speculations of a man of letters in his study; which produce no concrete effect, and which are of no other consequence to him except perhaps that the further they are away from common sense, the more vanity he will derive from them, because he will have had to use that much more skill and subtlety in order to make them seem dialectically probable. (1934, I, pp. 86–7)

The moral to draw is obvious. We may expect everyday and practically oriented perceptual judgements to be, typically, correct. But, at least initially, speculations either about another world, or about the operations of unobservables in this world, must be in prudence suspect. The reason is this. Whereas the price of your failing to perceive – say – advancing traffic will likely be immediate injury or death; the incomparably more appalling penalty of eternal damnation is by you felt to be – understandably even if falsely – both remote and unsure.

In Part II Descartes goes on to provide a second and more decisive general reason for doubting all theological and eschatalogical claims; although, to no one's surprise, he does not make the particular implications explicit. It is a moral to be drawn from his own travels in both space and time. (In Part I he had observed, with reference to his own historical reading, that 'to converse with those of other centuries is almost the same as to travel'.) The crucial statement in Part II is this:

> ...having learnt from the time I was at school that there is nothing one can imagine so strange or so unbelievable that it has not been said by one or other of the philosophers; and since then, while travelling, having recognized that all those who hold opinions quite opposed to ours are not on that account barbarians or savages, but that many exercise as much reason as we do, or more; and, having considered how a given man, with his given mind, being brought up from childhood among the French or Germans becomes different from what he would be if he had always lived among the Chinese or among cannibals; ... I was convinced that our beliefs are based much more on custom and example than on any certain knowledge... (1934, I. pp. 90–1)

For an attempt to point the general theological morals which Descartes was too discreet to draw, see Flew 1985.

1 Myself essentially a thinking substance

Immediately after the devastating sentence quoted at the end of the first paragraph of this present chapter, Descartes proceeds to pick out what alone appears to remain of rock-solid certainty: 'But immediately afterwards I noticed that whilst I thus wished to think all things false, it was absolutely essential that the "I" who thought this should be somewhat. . . ." Hence 'this truth, "I think therefore I am" became so certain and so assured that all the most extravagant suppositions brought forward by the sceptics were incapable of shaking it. . .' (1934, I, p. 101).

So what is this 'I' which Descartes is now sure that he can without further hesitation accept as the first principle of his new philosophy? He answers in the following paragraph:

. . .examining attentively that which I was, I saw that I could conceive that I had no body, and that there was no world nor place where I might be; but yet that I could not for all that conceive that I was not. . .From that I knew that I was a substance the whole essence or nature of which is to think, and for its existence there is no need of any place, nor does it depend on any material thing; so that this 'me', that is to say, the soul by which I am what I am, is entirely distinct from body, and is even more easy to know that is the latter; and even if body were not, the soul would not cease to be what it is. (I, p. 101)

(i) It is important to recognize that for Descartes the word 'thought' has, officially, a much wider than usual signification. It covers, not only the activity in which Rodin's *Le Penseur* is engaged, but also the enjoying or not enjoying of any and every form of consciousness – including the suffering of pains which may make ratiocination impossible. This comes out most clearly in a later work, *The Principles of Philosophy*. There, in Principle IX of Part I, (1934, I, p. 222; and compare Kenny 1970, p. 51), Descartes writes:

By the word 'thought' I understand all that of which we are conscious as operating in us. And that is why not alone understanding, willing, imagining, but also feeling, are here the same thing as thought. For if I say I see, or I walk, I therefore am, and if by seeing and walking I mean the action of my eyes or my legs, which is the work of my body, my conclusion is not absolutely certain; because it may be that, as often happens in sleep, I think I see or I walk, although I never open my eyes or move from my place, and the same thing perhaps might occur if I had not a body at all.

In thus identifying thought, and hence the mind, with consciousness Descartes was in effect introducing a fresh criterion of the
mental. Successors who had accepted this criterion were, therefore,
entirely right to dismiss all talk of the unconscious mind as, in
their own understanding, flatly self-contradictory. Where, of
course, they were wrong was in not appreciating that colleagues
talking in this way were employing a different criterion, which
they wished to recommend as heuristically more fertile. More
immediately relevant, the introduction of this fresh criterion: first
posed the problem of providing some account of the relations or
lack of relations between the two radically different worlds of stuff
and of consciousness; and then, after Newton, suggested that there
might be room for what Hume was to attempt to construct – a
kind of para-mechanics of the latter (Flew 1986a, ch. 8).

(ii) We are now in position to distinguish the three major
presuppositions which Descartes believes that he has established
by the end of the second paragraph of Part IV of the *Discourse*.
It was in order to make the nature and provenance of these three
fundamentals absolutely clear that we have been retraversing in
a leisurely way what is, presumably, very familiar ground. It is
however, scarcely possible to exaggerate the importance of this
enterprise. For, for nearly three centuries following the original
publication of this slim volume, all the greatest successors of that
bold French cavalier appear to have accepted all these first
conclusions as 'obvious dictates of reason', which 'no man, who
reflects, ever doubted'; although it was to only one of them Hume
himself directed these explicit words ([1748] XII.i, p. 152). It
is as true of both Hume and Kant as it is of Locke and Berkeley.
Already at the end of chapter five we saw how the same apparently
unquestionable presupppositions have in our own century inhibited
Popper. They take their heavy toll too not only in the epistemological writings of Bertrand Russell but also, equally clearly, in
the Ayer of *Language, Truth and Logic* and *The Foundations of
Empirical Knowledge*.

So what are these principles? First, in order of appearance in
Descartes, comes the complex idea that knowledge is possible only
when it is inconceivable that there might be error, or – very

much more weakly – when any denial of the proposition known must involve self-contradiction; and, hence, that no knowledge claim can be adequately vindicated by offering any evidencing reason for belief which does not actually entail the truth of the proposition asserted as known. Although this principle, or these principles, are rarely, if ever, both formulated clearly and boldly proclaimed, it has, or they have, continued to guide or to misguide philosophers, and not philosophers only, ever since Descartes tacitly appealed to it, or to them, in that first paragraph of Part IV of the *Discourse*.

It should by now be easy to see that this is indeed the appeal which was being made. Let us waive what is for us the peripheral objection that Descartes appears to be appealing to knowledge of the detection of previous mistakes in order to support the supposition that knowledge is, in the areas of these mistakes, altogether impossible. For there is no question but that the Cartesian case for extreme scepticism does depend upon this first assumption. Consider, for instance, the way in which it was made in the *Principles*, in the course of defining the word 'thought'. 'Because it may be that, as often happens in sleep, I think I see or I walk, although I never open my eyes or move from my place', no conclusion in any way based upon such sensory experience is 'absolutely certain', or, what presumably amounts to the same thing, truly known. Yet the only reason, or reasons, either offered or available for maintaining such scepticism is, or are, that error is here conceivable, and that the statement that it seemed to people that they perceived something does not entail that they actually did.

The second of these three fundamental principles is derived from the first. In resolving, 'since all the same thoughts and conceptions which we have while awake may come to us in sleep, . . . to assume that everything that ever entered into my mind was no more true than the illusions of my dreams', Descartes was proposing to take it that we are never immediately and non-inferentially aware of anything outside and independent of ourselves (I, p. 101). We are instead immediately and non-inferentially aware only of successive moments of our logically private consciousness. To employ more picturesque language: we are each and all of us separately and individually shut off from any External World which may or may not exist; for it is in any case necessarily and for ever hidden behind an impenetrable Veil of Appearance.

The third principle, as we have seen already, is that – essentially – we are incorporeal thinking substances; in the made-to-measure Cartesian understanding of 'thinking'. Although we are given an argument proceeding from premises stating what is and is not supposed to be conceivable, this third assumption can also be derived from the first and second, much as the second so obviously is in its turn derivable from the first. The nub of the matter is that the answer to Gilbert Ryle's question, 'What is the External World external to?', has to begin with an equally Rylean phrase, 'the Ghost in the Machine'. For in Cartesian terms all bodies, including human bodies, must be elements in the External World. Or – if a more epistemological formulation is preferred – if we are indeed for ever confined to an immediate awareness only of our own logically private consciousness, and if statements about that private consciousness can never possess sufficient logical strength to entail any conclusions about a mind-independent public world, then none of us could ever know that he or she – as the Platonic–Cartesian would have us say – *possesses a body*. (What should be said is that none of us could ever know that he or she *is a creature of flesh and blood*; or, perhaps, anything else at all.)

It is perhaps just worth pointing out that the phrase 'he or she' is quite inappropriate. For an incorporeal something could not have a sex; or, in the fashionable perverse misusage, a gender. (To the extent that gender, in the grammarian's traditional sense, is not necessarily related to sex an incorporeal person perhaps could have a gender!)

Since the three interlocking Cartesian conclusions, distinguished in this present section 1, are far more often followed than formulated, a summary restatement is in order. First, we have the assumption that all arguments must be either deductive or defective, since the only sufficient reasons for believing any proposition are (other) propositions which entail it. Second, there is the notion that we are (all of us) forever imprisoned behind Veils of Appearance, since we can never be immediately aware of any mind-independent realities. Third, and finally, it is argued or assumed that we essentially are incorporeal subjects of (only) the limited and ingrown sort of experience admitted under the second of these three principles.

2 Three consequences of incorporeality

By far the most important perceived consequences of these first Cartesian conclusions is the natural immortality of the human soul. Already in November 1630, in a letter to Father Mersenne, Descartes had written, with reference to what was presumably a draft for the *Discourse*: 'I set out principally to prove the existence of God and of our souls when they are separate from the body, from which their immortality follows' (Kenny 1970, p. 19). He was in those final five words perhaps putting it somewhat strong. Yet there can be no question but that it is here the first step of separate survival which counts, or costs – in the sense of being the hardest to effect.

In 1637, at the end of Part V of the *Discourse* as published, Descartes remarks that

next to the error of those who deny God, . . . there is none which is more effective in leading feeble spirits from the straight path of virtue, than to imagine that the souls of the brutes are of the same nature as our own; and that, in consequence, we have nothing to fear or to hope for after this life, any more than have ants and flies.

In fact, he insists, the differences are huge. They 'go to prove that our souls are in their natures entirely independent of bodies, and consequently not liable to die with them' (I, p. 118). In another letter to Mersenne, written in 1640 and referring to the manuscript of the *Meditations*, Descartes explains exactly what he does and does not claim to prove: 'I could not prove that God could not annihilate the soul but only that it is by nature entirely distinct from the body, and hence that it is not bound by nature to die with it' (Kenny 1970, p. 87).

There are, however, other passages which suggest a measure

of ambivalence. Certainly Descartes always takes pleasure in presenting his official account of the substantially dualistic nature of man – so aptly nicknamed the Ghost in the Machine story (Ryle 1949). In that account he argues that the incorporeal yet substantial mind or soul must be lodged in the *conarion* or pineal gland – a single unduplicated feature of the brain – there both receiving information input and, as it were, pulling levers to control the movements of the bodily machine. The entire distinctness asserted here is nevertheless sometimes qualified – or, some might object, contradicted – by an insistence that the 'entirely distinct' must somehow be 'more intimately joined and united'. Thus, immediately before the sentences quoted in our previous paragraph, Descartes writes 'that it would not suffice to place the soul in the human body, as a pilot in a ship, . . . but that it must be more intimately joined and united with the body in order to have feelings and appetites like ours, and so constitute a real man' (I, p. 118).

It is, however, in later years that Descartes perhaps makes his closest approach to abandoning a dualist, Platonic–Cartesian in favour of a monistic, Aristotelian conception of the nature of man; although it remains very far from clear what he thought he was saying in the passages in question. Writing to Princess Elizabeth of Bohemia on 21 May 1643, he reveals that our notion of the soul's power to move the body depends upon our having the notion of their union (Kenny 1970, p. 138). By this dark illumination Descartes may or may not have meant that, when a man moves his hand, he moves it immediately. He does not, that is to say, first bring about a purely mental event – a volition: a mental event the occurrence of which then causes the bodily movement. Thus there is no 'willing': no purely mental action which he performs directly in order to bring about the movement of his hand indirectly, as moving his hand may be what he does directly in order to move something else indirectly.

But if this is indeed what Descartes meant then he certainly hit upon an excruciatingly obscure way of saying it, as he seems himself to have recognized. For he returned to the charge the next month, providing a gloss which is not much more illuminating than the original text. In another letter to the persistently inquiring

Princess Elizabeth, dated 28 June 1643, he wrote: 'It does not seem to me that the human mind is capable of conceiving at the same time the distinction and the union between body and soul, because for this it is necessary to conceive them as a single thing and at the same time to conceive them as two things; and this is absurd' (Kenny 1970, p. 142).

(i) One paradoxical consequence of the contention that I am essentially a subject of consciousness is that I necessarily cannot exist unconscious. This again is a consequence which Descartes recognized and admitted, yet could scarcely welcome: '...whatever constitutes the nature of a thing always belongs to it so long as it exists. So it would be easier for me to believe that the soul ceased to exist at the times when it is supposed to cease to think than to conceive that it could exist without thought' (Kenny 1970, p. 125). But what he prefers to say is that, although there are in fact no interruptions of our streams of consciousness, there are of course periods about which we are later able to remember little or nothing.

Notoriously, this was too much for Locke to swallow: 'I confess my self, to have one of those dull Souls, that doth not perceive it self always to contemplate *Ideas*, nor can conceive it any more necessary for the *Soul always to think*, than for the Body always to move...' (Locke, [1690] II.i.9, p. 108). Fine and dandy. But Locke should not, from that characteristically commonsensical start, have gone on to maintain: 'We know certainly by Experience, that we sometimes think, and thence draw this infallible Consequence, That there is something in us, that has a Power to think...' (pp. 108–9).

Far from being infallible, the inference proposed is fatally fallacious. For what we may immediately infer from the premise provided is: not, excitingly, that there is *something in us* which has a power to think; but, truistically and tediously, that *we ourselves* have a power to think. By making the invalid inference which he did make Locke unveiled an artificial and perhaps insoluble problem of personal identity. So long as we are prepared resolutely and inflexibly to insist that people are what we are, members of one particular species of flesh and blood organisms, there is for us no tormenting philosophical problem here.

The simple solution is that a person at time two was, in the primary sense, the same person as a person at time one if and only if the former has been materially continuous with the latter. (When we say that someone has become quite a different person since he joined the Army or went into general practice we are using the expression 'different person' in a secondary sense. Such statements do not deny but rather presuppose that, in the primary sense, he is still the same.)

Personal identity, in that primary sense, is of course not the sufficient though it is the necessary condition of just accountability.) The prisoner in the dock would be conclusively shown to have been the woman who committed the murder if – as could scarcely ever happen – witnesses to that crime had kept the murderer under continuous observation ever since, and are now testifying that the prisoner is indeed the person thus continuously observed. It is, therefore, quite wrong to speak of such material continuity as either the or a criterion of personal identity. For it is not a criterion. It is that of which any criterion must be a criterion. It is, that is to say, personal identity itself. (Of which much more, of course, later.)

What is so intractable is the problem of providing an account of the possible identification and reidentification of *selves*, construed as perhaps incorporeal entities: entities supposedly not us but 'in us'; and yet endowed with what would normally be thought to be *our* powers of thought and action. Both substance and serial 'theories of the self' appear equally unpromising. Advocates of the former have to excogitate some identifying characteristics to attribute to exotic substances hypothesized as possessing these familiar powers, while partisans of the latter need to find some means of bridging apparent or actual interruptions of consciousness. The unending saga *Other Minds* somewhere entertains the possibility that an unkindly visitor to a patient awaiting surgery might warn: 'You'll have the usual anaesthetics, and you won't afterwards remember a thing. But you are going to feel everything, just as if anaesthetics had never been invented. I thought you'd want to know!' (Wisdom 1952). Had Locke lived after that invention, he could have exploited this thought experiment to shake complacencies about experiences had and to be had but not remembered.

(ii) The second paradoxical consequence of the third of these first Cartesian contentions is that everyone is alleged to be equipped with a concept of a substantial but incorporeal subject of consciousness. Were this true it would surely have come as a surprise to some of the Fathers of his Church. St Justin Martyr, for instance, in his 'Dialogue with Trypho', confesses that even 'philosophers cannot tell what a soul is' (ch. 5). St Jerome too described this supposedly unperplexing and universally familiar concept as 'one of the greatest problems with which the Church has to deal' (Letter 126, paragraph 5).

A more recent source is *Appearance and Reality*. Although Bradley never fairly considers the crudely commonsensical contention that people are members of a particular species of flesh and blood organisms, he is eager to ridicule any assumption that we can all, nevertheless, clearly and distinctly conceive of our selves (two words; compare Flew 1950a and the Locke quotation at p. 99, above). 'A man,' Bradley begins, 'commonly thinks that he knows what he means by his self' (1897, p. 75). However, 'so far is the self from being clearer than things outside us that, to speak generally, we never know what we mean when we talk of it' (p. 76). So Bradley goes on to draw impeccable conclusions:

We have been led up to the problem of personal identity, and any one, who thinks that he knows what he means by his self, may be invited to solve this...The true cause of failure lies in this – that we will persist in asking questions when we do not know what they mean, and when their meaning perhaps presupposes what is false...the main point is to fix the meaning of person; and it is chiefly because our ideas as to this are confused, that we are unable to come to a further result. (p. 81)

The first step in the argument which Descartes offers for this second paradoxical conclusion is perfectly sound. It is put most persuasively in a letter to Mersenne, answering a correspondent who 'could not understand, as he says, what I mean by the idea of God, the idea of the soul, and the ideas of imperceptible things' (Kenny 1970, p. 105). Descartes replies that he means

...by the idea of God nothing but what all men habitually understand when they speak of Him...In the case of the soul the matter is even clearer. As I have shown, the soul is nothing but a thing which thinks, and so it is impossible for us ever to think of anything without at the same time having the idea of our soul as a thing capable of thinking of whatever we think of. (p. 106)

Suppose that we dismiss two immediate objections as not crucially relevant: first, the objection that any relative superiority in the Cartesian concept of soul arises from the still greater unclarity and indeterminateness of popular notions of God (Flew 1985); and, second, the objection that – in the official, extended, Cartesian sense of 'thinking' – the brutes too must be presumed to be in their waking hours, without being possessed of any concepts at all, forever engaged in thinking. Then we must surely allow that, for anyone to know any proposition the subject of which is a personal pronoun, they have to know both the meaning and the reference of that subject term. Where Descartes goes wrong is in conjoining this perfectly correct contention with his account of persons as incorporeal souls, the substantial subjects of purely private experience. As such, Descartes maintains, he is a substance the whole essence or nature of which is to think...so that this "me", that is to say, the soul by which I am what I am, is entirely distinct from body, and is even more easy to know than is the latter; and even if the body were not the soul would not cease to be what it is' (Descartes 1934, I, p. 101).

(iii) The third of our present three paradoxical consequences is little more than a statement or restatement of the third of the three first Cartesian conclusions. It is that people are essentially incorporeal. Frequently philosophers fail to appreciate that this consequence is in any degree paradoxical. They are prepared to ask themselves, without either blushing or blinking, whether immaterial persons are one of the possible sorts of which there conceivably might exist specimens; there are even those who will categorically insist that they are. Thus Roland Puccetti, in his exciting book *Persons: A Study of Possible Moral Agents in the Universe*, discusses the claim that 'a person *necessarily* has corporeal attributes as well as other kinds of attributes' (Strawson 1959, p. 132). Against this Puccetti maintains that a satisfactorily non-revisionist 'characterization must, for example, exclude dogs, but leave room for God' (1968, p. 4; and compare Abelson 1977, p. 87).

Defying charges of Revisionism – which appear to be almost as grave here as among the fundamentalists of Marxism – we have to respond that this argument ought to be reversed. If to admit the legitimacy of a concept of God as an immaterial person warrants the conclusion that persons can coherently be described as incorporeal, then that, surely, becomes a knockdown decisive reason for denying that the premise concept is indeed legitimate (Flew 1976a, ch. 1 and 1985)?

It is, therefore, significant that in *The Coherence of Theism*, the first leg of his theological tripos, Richard Swinburne starts by arguing: 'that it certainly does not follow from the fact that the only ϕ's we have ever seen are ψ that it is not coherent to suppose that there are ϕ's which are not ψ' (1977, p. 54). This is, of course, correct: certainly it might have been that all the people whom some nineteenth-century African ever met had black skins; and it would indeed in that case have been wrong for him to argue that a black or any other particular colour of skin must be essential to humanity. Nevertheless it is almost comical to employ this argument, as Swinburne does, interpreting ϕ's as people and ψ as corporeality. For here we have a very different kettle of fish; or, more like it, no kettle and no fish. To characterize something as incorporeal is to make an assertion which is at one and the same time both extremely comprehensive and wholly negative. Those proposing to do this surely owe it both to themselves and to others: not only to indicate what positive characteristics might significantly be attributed to their putative incorporeal entities; but also to specify how such entities could, if only in principle, be identified and reidentified. What sorts of predicates can these supposed subjects take, and to just what are any attributes proposed as possible to be attributed?

It is only later, in a chapter entitled 'An Omnipresent Spirit', that Swinburne attends more closely to the problem of identifying and reidentifying persons. His attention there is in fact almost exclusively on reidentification as the same person, rather than on the logically prior question of the original identification. On the reidentification issue, arguing against Terence Penelhum, Swinburne takes it that the objection to giving an account of the identity of putatively disembodied persons in terms of memory claims is that such claims could not be checked; which he contends that they could be. But the decisive objection, put so perfectly by Bishop Butler, is that true memory presupposes, and therefore cannot constitute, personal identity. When I truly remember doing that, what I remember is that I am the same person as did it; that I am the person who did it (Butler 1896, I, p. 388).

From here Swinburne proceeds, by way of another false and this time surely fatal step, to argue 'that the identity of a person over time is something ultimate, not analysable in terms of bodily continuity or continuity of memory or character' (1977, p. 110). The fatal step is to assume that, in our dealings with the ordinary flesh and blood persons which we all are, 'we may use bodily continuity to reach conclusions about personal identity' (p. 109). For what we use bodily criteria for is to establish bodily continuity. And this is not just a usually reliable criterion for, but a large part if not the whole of what is meant by, personal identity. (It would be, wouldn't it, if persons just are, as I maintain that we all know that we are, specimens of a very special sort of creatures of flesh and blood?)

There is, however, so far no call to deny that it might be not only possible but even desirable to construct some compassable sense for the expression 'bodiless person'; just as it should not surpass the wit of man to think up a meaning for the term 'God' which would be adequate to ensure that the question whether the corresponding concept of God does in fact have an object is straightforwardly decidable. Yet to make these two concessions is not to say: either that, in the established understanding of person-words – the understanding which determines the true answers to existential questions about personal identity, and hence individual responsibilities and individual expectations – any putative bodiless persons could or should be identified with any of us ordinary people; or that any traditional and widely favoured conception of God is in fact so structured as to satisfy the modest requirements for empirical applicability.

If it is to make sense to suggest that there might actually be some of these bodiless persons, then the provision of meaning for the expression 'bodiless person' has to include indications of how, in principle at least, they are to be identified and reidentified. The parallelism between questions about the yet to be constructed concept of a bodiless (human) person and questions about the traditional conception of God as an immaterial person merits further attention. For the failure to provide an adequate response to the demand for the means by which its putative object might be identified and reidentified must be, surely, at least part of the explanation of the perennial persistence of dispute as to whether such a concept does indeed have actual application? Again it is, or should be, notorious that theologians have had difficulty: not only in indicating how the subject of all their discourse is to be identified as a persistent object (Kaufmann 1959, and Hepburn 1963; compare Hampshire 1959, ch. 1); but also in excogitating humanly intelligible positive attributes with which they would themselves be content to endow their postulated Great Subject (Flew 1966, ch. 2).

Sir Peter Strawson has been charged with incontinently constructing his account of persons from 'noticeably Cartesian materials . . . Neither Strawson nor Descartes shows much disposition to relate persons to any classification of living things . . . The neglect of the continuity of our ascriptions of predicates to human beings and to other animals is bound to produce an artificial (and highly Cartesian) dichotomy between persons and everything else' (Williams 1973, p. 66). It also leads to a willingness to entertain the suggestion that disembodiment is for persons, though not of course for the brutes, a possible if unappealing and ultimately destructive fate.

In both versions of the Strawson account the fundamental contention is that persons are tokens of 'a type of entity such that *both* predicates ascribing states of consciousness *and* predicates ascribing corporeal characteristics... are equally applicable to an individual entity of that type' (Strawson 1958, pp. 342–3; and compare Strawson 1959, p. 102). Yet by enunciating this basic proposition Strawson disqualifies himself from later saying, as in his second and presumably more polished version he does later say, that 'each of us can quite intelligibly conceive of his or her individual survival of bodily death. The effort of imagination is not even great' (Strawson 1959, p. 115).

Really to imagine myself disembodied would surely have to be to imagine (the same person as) me; but disembodied. Now, either we really imagine a person or we do not. *'Former* persons' (*Ibid.*, 1959, p. 116), if they are only *former* persons, are no more a sort of persons than *ex*-wives, if they are only *ex*-wives, are a sort of wives. We cannot, therefore, allow Strawson these concluding manoeuvres: first, in his easy imaginings, assuming that his putative desembodied beings would be persons; and then, when the going gets tougher, sidestepping the consequent charge of inconsistency by maintaining that they are only *former*, and hence after all not really and fully, *persons*.

To conclude the chapter on a modestly technical yet mildly mischievous note, we can put the crucial point in this way: in expressions such as 'bodiless person' or 'disembodied person' the adjectives are alienans adjectives; like 'positive' in 'positive freedom', or 'People's' in People's Democracy' (Flew 1983). Hobbes put the same point with a characteristically brutal verve in chapter IV of his *Leviathan*: 'insignificant sounds,' he concluded, are 'of two sorts. One when they are new, and yet their meaning not explained. . . Another, when men make a name of two names, whose significations are contradictory and insignificant; as this name, an *incorporeal body*, or, which is all one, an *incorporeal substance*, and a great number more' (1961, III, p. 27).

Chapter Seven
Personal Identity: (i) Conceivable Differences?

> But fundamentally an organism has conscious mental states if
> and only if there is something that it is like to *be* that
> organism – something it is like *for* the organism.
>
> Thomas Nagel, 'What is it like to be a bat?' (1974), p. 392

> I can *imagine* myself existing without a body. I know, in
> other words, *what it would be like* to exist without a body. I
> imagine that I see the same visual field as I am seeing now,
> but cannot see or touch anything which I would call 'my
> body', and have no bodily sensations; at the same time I
> remember various events which happened in my 'embodied'
> life, feel certain emotions, and have a continuous train of
> thought. I can, that is to say, imagine a situation that would
> *verify* that I have survived the death of my body.
>
> Casimir Lewy, 'Is the notion of disembodied existence
> self-contradictory?' (1942–3), pp. 64–5

It is curious that Hobbes, who not only in *Leviathan* but also in
earlier works is so emphatic in his rejection of all talk of immaterial
or incorporeal bodies as self-contradictory, refrains in his Objections to the *Meditations* from making this point directly. Instead
he prefers to argue that Descartes has failed to prove his own
contrary contention, while merely suggesting that and why he
himself believes that it never could be proved. Hobbes takes as
his premise 'that we can conceive no activity whatsoever apart

from its subject, e.g. we cannot think of leaping apart from that which leaps, of knowing apart from a knower, or of thinking apart from a thinker' (Descartes 1934, II, p. 62).

1   Contemporary objections to the Cartesian Conceivability Contention

Hobbes then proceeds, with uncharacteristic moderation: 'It seems to follow that that which thinks is something corporeal; for, as it appears, the subjects of all activities can be conceived only after a corporeal fashion... as M. Descartes himself afterwards shows, when he illustrates by means of wax...' (Descartes 1934, II, p. 62). M. Descartes thought little of 'the paper written by the Englishman', and hoped to see it off in very short order, 'since his objections seemed to implausible to me that to answer them at greater length would have been giving them too much importance' (Kenny 1970, pp. 91 and 100). It is obvious from these answers that Descartes failed to realize just how deep was the radicalism of this solitary, cross-grained British objector: '...both logicians and as a rule all men are wont to say that substances are of two kinds, spiritual and corporeal' (II, p. 63). No doubt; but neither on this nor on any other matter was Hobbes one to follow the crowd.

(i) In *Meditation* VI Descartes elucidates the distinction between imagining, in the sense of imaging, and conceiving, in a fashion so clear and so memorable that we might have dared to hope that it would never again be collapsed by any of his successors:

But I cannot image the thousand sides of a chiliagon as I do the three sides of the triangle... And although... it may happen that in conceiving a chiliagon I do confusedly represent some figure to myself; still it is very clear that this figure is not a chiliagon, since it does not differ at all from the one which I should represent to myself if I were thinking of a myriagon or of any other many sided figure; not does it serve my purpose in discovering the properties which go to form the difference between a chiliagon and other polygons. (I, p. 186)

To support his claim that he is an incorporeal thinking substance Descartes urges only the weaker thesis that such existence is conceivable, not that it is a way of life of which he can also form images. In the *Discourse* the choice of mood for the last verb is a little strange, suggesting that we have here a report of the unsurprising discovery that merely to suppose myself destroyed is not in itself fatal: 'I saw that I could conceive that I had no body, and that there was no world nor place where I might be; but yet that I could not for all that conceive that I was not' (I, p. 101).

(ii) Even when sympathetically and constructively reinterpreted this statement amounts to no more than a bald and categorical assertion that the supposition of bodiless personal existence is coherent and perfectly intelligible. In the fourth set of Objections Antoine Arnauld, later to become the chief author of the *Port-Royal Logic*, begins by noticing some Augustinian anticipations. From a firm though gentle insistence that this statement 'in the Method' gets us nowhere, Arnauld proceeds to point out that *Meditation* II is still no help: 'The problem is: how it follows, from the fact that one is unaware that anything else [save to be a thinking thing] belongs to one's essence, that nothing else belongs to one's essence' (Descartes 1934, II, p. 81).

The ensuing discussion does nothing to solve that problem; for the simple and sufficient reason that it is not soluble. His tentative politeness notwithstanding, the young Arnauld had well and truly caught Descartes; who was indeed here committing the Larvatus, or Masked Man, Fallacy. If the masked man is someone whose identity I do not know, and my father is not someone whose identity I do not know, it does not follow that the masked man is not my father; only that I do not know him to be. (It may have been a Freudian self-betrayal which once led Descartes to write in his private notebook 'larvatus prodeo' [I come forward wearing a mask]: see Geach 1969, p. 8.)

2 The Imaginability Thesis

The alternative tactic for those aspiring to sustain the same conclusion is to argue, or – more commonly – brashly to assert as a manifest and inexpugnable certainty, that our own disembodied personal existence is not merely a conceivable but also an imaginable possibility. Such a conviction is the more striking when it is found, as it so often is, in lifelong mortalists. Among the classical philosophers the most remarkable case is that of David Hume. For, although his essay 'Of the Immortality of the Soul' was published only posthumously, there is no doubt but that he was converted to mortalism at a very early age. Yet even he – even what Gilbert Ryle so loved to call 'the ungullible Hume' – never, it seems, thought to challenge this Cartesian contention. In his *Treatise* the section 'Of the immateriality of the soul' immediately precedes that 'Of personal identity'; where his difficulties arise precisely because he refuses to recognize that we persons are not immaterial souls but creatures of sometimes all too solid flesh (Flew 1986a, ch. 6).

(i) Still more remarkable is the fact that leading contemporary philosophers, who are in their eschatological convictions no less mortalist than Hume, continue to repeat the same confident claim, the claim that they can imagine their own disembodied survival. They are, apparently, entirely unaware that this claim has ever been seriously challenged. Yet, when they confidently remake it, it is significant that their own supporting formulations are often insufficient to sustain the desired conclusion.

Strawson, for instance, makes a bad start by simultaneously not only collapsing the so carefully made Cartesian distinction between conceiving and imagining (imaging) but also forgetting his own insistence that persons are tokens of 'a type of entity such that *both* predicates ascribing states of consciousness *and* predicates ascribing corporeal characteristics ... are equally applicable to an individual of that single type' (Strawson 1959, p. 102: emphasis original). He claims that:

from within our actual conceptual scheme, each of us can quite intelligibly conceive of his or her individual survival of bodily death. The effort of imagination is not even great. One has simply to think of oneself as having thoughts and memories as at present ... whilst (a) having no perceptions of a body related to one's experience as one's own body is, and (b) having no power of initiating changes in the physical condition of the world, such as one at present does with one's hands, shoulders, feet and vocal chords. (1959, p. 115)

Certainly it is true that 'from within our actual conceptual scheme', each of us can quite intelligibly conceive of being in the situation described in Strawson's final sentence above: 'One has simply to think of oneself as having thoughts and memories as at present. . .' and so on. But this description is, as far as it goes, a description of a (flesh and blood) patient afflicted by both a total paralysis and a very peculiar perceptual disorder. So all that Strawson has here succeeded in doing is to erect one more butt for the objection first raised in section 1 of Chapter one above: that to suggest 'that after my death and dissolution such things might happen to me is to overlook that I shall not then exist. To expect such things, through overlooking this, is surely like accepting a fairy tale as history, through ignoring the prefatory rubric: "Once upon a time, in a world that never was. . ."'?'

Again, Sir Alfred Ayer claimed in his Gifford Lectures: 'One can imagine oneself waking to find oneself deprived of any bodily feeling or any perception of one's own body; one can imagine oneself seeming to wander round the world like a ghost, intangible to others and only occasionally visible. . ., a spectator of a world in which one does not participate' (Ayer 1973, p. 124).

Even a still more recent book, *The Miracle of Theism*, proclaiming from the beginning that it will be reaching atheist conclusions, has neither fundamental doubts about *The Coherence of Theism*, nor problems with bodiless personal existence: 'Although all the persons we are acquainted with have bodies, there is no great difficulty in conceiving what it would be for there to be a person without a body: for example, one can imagine oneself surviving without a body, and, while at present one can act and produce results only by using one's limbs or one's speech organs, one can *imagine* having one's intentions fulfilled directly, without such physical means' (Mackie 1982, pp. 1–2, emphasis original, and compare Swinburne 1977).

Before going any further, two minor concessions can and

therefore must be made: first, to Ayer, that 'one can imagine oneself... deprived of any bodily feeling or any perception of one's own body'; and, second, to Mackie that 'one can *imagine* having one's intentions fulfilled directly, without...physical means'. Indeed one can. But this shows no more than that neither Ayer nor Mackie thought their theses through. For in neither case has the 'oneself' involved been explicitly specified as incorporeal. The first stipulation, as Ayer actually formulates it here, could be satisfied, and perhaps sometimes in fact is, by some dully corporeal patient. The second could serve as a description of the putative phenomenon of psychokinesis, a.k.a. PK (Flew 1987, II 2(5)). Certainly, genuine PK performers are excessively hard to find. But this, so to speak, systematic elusiveness has to be put down not to their incorporeality but to the fact that PK capacities are rare to the point of non-existence.

A position similar to those of Casimir Lewy, Ayer and Mackie was taken much earlier by Moritz Schlick, founder member and chairman of the old original Vienna Circle of Logical Positivists: 'I take it for granted...we are concerned with the question of survival after "death". I think we may agree with Professor C. I. Lewis when he says about this hypothesis: "Our understanding of what would verify it has no lack of clarity".' (Notice, by the way, that it was Schlick himself who inserted those giveaway inverted commas round the word 'death' in his first sentence. They constitute a tacit admission that the expression 'to survive death' is indeed self-contradictory. Compare the similar tacit concession in the tombstone protest: 'Not dead, but sleeping'.) Schlick continued:

In fact I can easily imagine, e.g. witnessing the funeral of my own body and continuing to exist without a body, for nothing is easier than to describe a world which differs from our ordinary world only in the complete absence of all data which I would call parts of my own body. We must conclude that immortality, in the sense defined, should not be regarded as a metaphysical 'problem', but as an empirical hypothesis, because it possesses logical verifiability. It could be verified by following the prescription 'Wait until you die!' (Schlick 1937 and 1949, pp. 356 and 159–60)

A more puckishly picturesque version was later provided by Wisdom himself: 'I know indeed what it would be like to witness my own funeral – the men in tall silk hats, the flowers, and the face beneath the glass-topped coffin' (Wisdom 1952, p. 36).

(ii) So far as I know, this Imaginability Thesis was not challenged in print until twenty years after the first appearance of Schlick's paper (Flew 1956; and compare Williams 1966, p. 40). Although this challenge, under the catchpenny title 'Can a man witness his own funeral?', has been reprinted five or six times, it appears that so far no one has made any sustained or systematic attempt to meet it. Presumably the reasons why twenty years were allowed to pass before anyone stepped forward to make such a challenge were: first, that we can – most of us – imagine (image) a scene such as Wisdom describes; and, second, that no one wants to arrogate to himself the right to decide what Wisdom or Schlick or anyone other than he himself can or cannot imagine (image). Nevertheless it is a thesis which can and should be challenged, and the challenge can be pressed home without presuming to draw limits to Wisdom's no doubt extensive powers of private mental picturing. The crux is that there is a world of difference between: on the one hand, imagining what it would be like to witness my own funeral; and, on the other hand, imagining what it would be like *for me* to witness my own funeral. What Schlick and Wisdom and everyone else can certainly do is the former. What would be needed to warrant Schlick's conclusions is the latter. The question at issue is a question about possible pictures and possible captions. Everyone knows what picture fits the first caption. What picture is it which fits, and justifies, the second caption?

If it is really I who witness, then it is not my funeral but only 'my funeral' (in inverted commas). If it really is my funeral, then I cannot be a witness; since I shall be dead and in the coffin. Of course I can imagine (image) what might be described as my watching 'my own funeral' (in inverted commas). I can remember Harry Lime in the film *The Third Man* watching 'his own funeral', and of course I can imagine being in the same situation as Harry Lime. But it was not really Harry Lime's own funeral, and what

I can imagine would not really be mine. Again I can imagine my own funeral – I shall not try to better Wisdom's whimsical description of such a scene. But now what I am imagining is not my witnessing my own funeral but merely my own funeral.

It is interesting to notice that, just as Schlick gave a trick away by his nicely sensitive insertion of the required inverted commas round the word 'death', so Wisdom likewise is too careful a stylist to allow one of his characters to describe his imagings in the terms needed to support the Imaginability Thesis. What Wisdom wrote was: 'I know indeed what it would be like to witness my own funeral.' But this does nothing to support the disputed thesis. What that requires is that he should be able to imagine his surviving his own death and his witnessing his own funeral. For it is this which Schlick's opponent maintains is a self-contradictory suggestion, and hence strictly incoherent.

But surely, someone will object, all this is merely cheap and flash? Surely you can perfectly well imagine your own funeral, really your own funeral with your body in the coffin and not a substitute corpse or a weight of bricks; with you there watching it all, but invisible, intangible, a disembodied spirit? Well, yes, this seems all right – until someone asks the awkward question: 'Just how does all this differ from your imagining your own funeral without your being there at all (except as the corpse in the coffin)?'

Certainly Schlick could imagine, as he claimed, 'the funeral of his own body', although it is perhaps a pity that he should describe what he imaged in this fashion, instead of speaking in a more natural and less misleading way, of his own funeral. But then he goes on to talk of his 'continuing to exist without a body', which he tried to justify by claiming that 'nothing is easier than to describe a world which differs from our ordinary world only in the complete absence of all data which I would call parts of my own body'. But the fact that we can all of us describe, or even imagine, a world which would differ from our ordinary world only in the complete absence of all data describable as parts of our respective bodies has not, by itself, the slightest tendency to show that anyone could imagine or describe a world in which, after his funeral, he continued to exist without a body. By itself it merely shows that we can each imagine what the world would be like if we were obliterated from it entirely, and no trace of our corpses remained.

(iii) We have in challenging the Imaginability Thesis been following a recommendation from *The Blue Book*: 'We could perfectly well, for our purposes, replace every process of imagining by a process of looking at an object or by painting, drawing or modelling; and every process of speaking to oneself by speaking aloud or by writing' (Wittgenstein 1958, p. 4). But there is one important direction in which this recommendation has to be qualified: '. . . we have no simple ways of making models of organic sensations, feelings of vertigo, perplexity, intoxication and so forth. Hence the conventions of the comic strip cartoonists – stars, question and exclamation marks, whirling lines etc.' (Mace 1942–3, p. 22n). This point once grasped, we must also go on to notice the difference between two claims which Lewy mistook to be equivalent: 'I can imagine myself existing without a body. I know, *in other words*, what it would be like to exist without a body' (Lewy 1942–3, p. 64; emphasis changed).

It is not clear whether Schlick would have wanted to include bodily sensations under his rubric of 'all data which I would call parts of my own body', or whether he was thinking only of the visual and other sense-data involved in his directly or indirectly perceiving all or parts of his own body. (The 'or indirectly' goes in to allow for his seeing his face in the mirror while shaving, and the like.) On the other hand, it is perfectly plain that bodily sensations are exactly what was in mind when Ayer asked us to imagine 'oneself waking to find oneself deprived of any bodily feeling' and when Lewy wrote 'I imagine that I. . .have no bodily sensations'.

But all three went wrong here through proposing that we should imagine nothing but the absence of something: whether 'all data which I would call parts of my own body'; or 'any bodily feeling or any perception of one's own body.' If either the Cartesian Conceivability Contention or this stronger Imaginability Thesis is to be made out, then it has got to be shown that and how we can positively and directly conceive or imagine (image) something incorporeal, something incorporeal which would also be identifiable as us: us actually having such (bodiless) bodily sensations; as well as us doing or suffering at least some of the other things characteristically or exclusively done or suffered by people. What certainly will not do is to postulate any sort of 'perceptions of the mind' occurring 'loose and separate'. For it makes no more sense to speak of a pain or a sense-datum which was not suffered or had than it does to talk of grins and lost tempers apart from the creatures that grin or which lose their tempers. What has to be done is to provide some acceptable account of what it is which is supposed to be enjoying or suffering these postulated experiences.

Putting it with some restraint, it is far from obvious either how or, therefore, that this trick can be turned. However, once the point made in the previous paragraph it taken, it may begin to appear that there is rather more promise in an approach from the outside. Instead of asking first what it would be like to serve as a bodiless witness at our own or anybody else's funeral, perhaps we ought to begin by asking whether anything might induce us to attribute to something incorporeal the having of either (bodiless) bodily sensations, or (sense-organless) sense-data, or any other mind of consciousness; and just what would it be to which we might thus attribute these attributes.

Working on these lines, presumably the least bad bet would be first to imagine a voice regularly coming out of the air: either from always roughly the same place; or else changing position in some smoothly continuous way. If what the voice said suggested a single integrated personality, and if it made a convincing claim to be producing psychokinetic effects, then maybe we should find it hard not to attribute some sort of consciousness to an originating we know not what: 'Just try – in a real case – to doubt someone else's fear or pain' (Wittgenstein 1953, p. 102).

Yet it is 'a truth of the first importance', a truth enforced by the whole later work of the author of those *Philosophical Investigations*, 'that there is a conceptual connection between descriptions of creatures in mental terms and descriptions in behavioural terms' (Campbell 1970, pp. 74–5). In that imagined case we should have, as it were, behaviour; but with no discernible behaver: 'Only of what behaves like a human being can one say that it *has* pains.

For one has to say it of a body, or, if you like of a soul which some body *has.*' Yet what would there be to provide purchase for such attributions? As the same author says later: 'The human body is the best picture of the human soul' (Wittgenstein 1953, pp. 98 and 178).

Suppose that we did eventually satisfy ourselves in this enterprise. Then this success would perhaps have made it profitable to wonder what it would be like to *be* such an incorporeal subject of consciousness. Yet by then our labours would surely have taught us that this wondering must be in the last degree speculative and academic? Quite apart from all the conceptual difficulties of identifying any such incorporeal entity at time two with any particular individual human being at time one, we should be faced with the inescapable fact that we have absolutely no reason to believe that our Universe contains any such entities; entities with whom, or with which, previously existing human beings might be identified.

(iv) The first epigraph at the head of the present chapter insists that 'an organism has conscious mental states if and only if there is something that it is like to *be* that organism – something it is like *for* the organism'. It was that same fundamental and incomparably important fact to which the Prince of Denmark traced 'the dread of something after death', which

> . . .makes us rather bear those ills we have
> Than fly to others that we know not of?
> Thus conscience doth make cowards of us all.
> (*Hamlet*, III.i)

There is a general error here into which it is exceedingly easy to fall. That general error, of which the confusing of the experience of witnessing my own funeral with the experience of *my* witnessing my own funeral is a particular specimen of one special kind of case, is that of confounding what it would be like to be – say – a bat with what it would be like *for me* to be a bat.

The nerve of this fallacy consists in overlooking that my essential characteristics, whether as a person or as the particular person who I am, may be, and often are, incompatible with the equally essential characteristics of whoever or whatever it is who or what I am tempted to suppose that I might be or have been, might become or have become. It is one thing to wonder what it is like (for a bat) to be a bat. It is quite another to wonder what it would be like (for me) to be changed into a bat; but (inside) retaining the memories and the now entirely frustrated dispositions of the former Flew. (This second speculation parallels that of Franz Kafka's appalling and unforgettable *Metamorphosis* [1916]: 'As Gregor Samsa awoke one morning from uneasy dreams he found himself transformed in his bed into a gigantic insect.') Again, it is one thing to wonder what it was like to be Napoleon – the bridge at Arcola, the sun of Austerlitz, the flames of Moscow, Waterloo. . . It is quite another to deliberate about what *you* would have done if *you* had been Napoleon. For at least some of the facts of *your* parentage, *your* date and place of birth, and *your* upbringing – facts altogether inconsistent with any such might-have-been suppositions – must be recognized not as contingent but necessary truths about your own unique individuality (Kripke 1980).

3 Personal identity and material continuity

Throughout the present book it has again and again been emphasized that everyone's paradigms of what persons are are members of our own particular species of flesh and blood organisms. Given a firm insistence upon this starting point there is, as was said in section 2 (i) of chapter six, 'no tormenting philosophical problem of personal identity here. The simple solution is that a person at time two was the same person as a person at time one if and only if the former has been materially continuous with the latter. . . the prisoner in the dock would be conclusively shown to have been the woman who committed the murder if witnesses to that crime had kept the murderer under continuous observation ever since, and are now testifying that the prisoner is indeed the person thus continuously observed.'

(i) Since most of the world's present population had not yet been born when I was an undergraduate studying philosophy in the University of Oxford, it may seem to many that this emphasis upon personal corporeality has been unnecessary, or at any rate excessive. Maybe it is true that 'all the great philosophical discoveries are discoveries of the obvious' (Price 1940, p. 12). But that does not make every reiteration of a truism a great philosophical discovery. When, however, in the early fifties, I first began to emphasize this particular truism it was in philosophical discussions of personal identity both largely and widely ignored (Flew 1950a, 1951a and b, 1953 and 1956a). Not only the classical readings from Locke, Berkeley, Butler and Hume, but also the contemporary articles recommended to students preparing essays on this topic, appeared to take it for granted that the problem was how to identify and reidentify potentially and hence, presumably, essentially bodiless subjects of consciousness. Certainly the two comparatively recent articles most often discussed were Ian Gallie's 'Is the Self a Substance?' (1936) and Paul Grice's 'Personal Identity' (1941); the latter a critique of Gallie's contribution from a serialist standpoint by one of my own two philosophy tutors. Even a dozen years later even Anthony — now Lord — Quinton was still writing in the same genre.

It was no doubt appreciation of the importance of this turn which led the author of the volume on *Personal Identity* in a series of introductions to 'Problems of Philosophy' to say that one of my articles from that period (Flew 195 1 b) 'marks a turning point in discussions of personal identity' (Vesey 1974, p. 112). Turning point it may have been, though surely not the kind after which progress is direct and continuous, with no turning back. For it can still be very respectably argued 'that the identity of a person over time is something ultimate, not analysable in terms of bodily continuity or continuity of memory and character' (Swinburne 1977, p. 110). With the problem of *The Coherence of Theism* still very much in mind the same author, in his contribution to a 'Great Debate' on this subect, is willing, even eager, to contend that there is 'no contradiction in the supposition that a person might acquire a totally new body (including a completely new brain) — as many religious accounts of life after death claim that men do' (Swinburne 1984, p. 22).

After this we can scarcely be surprised to hear it suggested: 'that there may be kinds of stuff other than matter'; or that, though 'a chunk of matter necessarily takes up a finite volume of space', still 'that kind of consideration has no application to immaterial stuff' (1984, pp. 27 and 28). Yet anyone familiar with the reasons why Hobbes was to his opponents in controversy known as 'the monster of Malmesbury' may perhaps be disappointed by the un-Hobbist restraint of the riposte in this particular debate. It is purely parenthetical and cautiously concessive: 'although speaking of immaterial stuff seems dangerously close to speaking of immaterial matter' (Shoemaker 1984, p. 125).

(ii) As has been recognized throughout the present work, the reason why so many philosophers are so reluctant to settle for corporeal continuity as the sufficient or even as one necessary condition of personal identity is: both that people have insides as well as outsides, in the sense that at least in our waking hours there is something which it is like to be us; and that – again at least in those hours – we are all in various ways conscious, as well as – from time to time – either rational or irrational This is the crucial fact of which due account is being taken when, at the beginning of a study under the suggestively reactionary title *Self-Knowledge and Self-Identity*, it is written 'that the existence of a special problem about the nature of persons, and the nature of personal identity, is somehow connected with the fact that persons have minds' (Shoemaker 1963, p. 8).

Philosophers are by other equally familiar facts further encouraged to believe that they can or must develop some account of the identity of personalities independent of any account of the identity of the people whom those personalities – shall we say? – characterize. These are the facts that two different people may have somewhat similar personalities, and that the same person may after some lapse of time seem to be characterized by a substantially different personality. It was, surely, Locke's attention to these further facts which persuaded him, in the course of the seminal discussion 'Of Identity and Diversity' in *An Essay concerning Human Understanding*, to try to make a distinction between 'man' and 'person'. He was further encouraged in this enterprise by entertaining several conceivable cases which suppose various changes much more drastic and abrupt than any which do in fact occur.

However, in the end, Locke seems to want to construe the word 'man' as referring to an organism of a particular kind endowed with a particular bundle of capacities and dispositions – very much as we have been construing 'person' – while detaching that latter word itself from any reference either to that or to any other kind of organism. In the development of this account there is at first no mention of anything but the shape and structure of the organism. Locke writes:

He that shall place the *Identity* of Man in anything else, but like that of other Animals in one fitly organized Body taken in any one instant, and from thence continued under one Organization of Life in several successive fleeting Particles of Matter, united to it, will find it hard, to make an *Embryo*, one of Years, mad, and sober, the same Man . . . ([1690] II.xxvii.7, pp. 331–2)

But then, after retailing a story of a rational parrot in Brazil, a story allegedly heard by 'an Author of great note . . . from *Prince Maurice's* own mouth', Locke seems to realize that, unless this first official definition is appropriately supplemented, we might have to admit as men creatures which, although organisms of the species Homo sapiens, or of one of the other species recognized as species of men, no one would want to count as human beings. He puts it the other way round: 'For I presume 'tis not the *Idea* of a thinking or rational Being alone, that makes the *Idea* of *Man* in most people's Sense; but of a Body so and so shaped joined to it . . .' (II.xxvii.8, pp. 333 and 335). If and in so far as his first official definition is amended to take account of this popular insight, men do indeed become 'organisms of a particular kind endowed with a particular bundle of capacities and dispositions'.

Locke then proceeds, always in accordance with his own much and correctly criticized account of meaning, to the next move: '. . . we must consider what *Person* stands for; which, I think, is a thinking intelligent being, that has reason and reflection, and can consider it self as it self, the same thinking thing in different times and places. . .' (II.xxvii.9, p. 335). On this definition people are neither — like men — essentially corporeal nor — like Cartesian thinking substances — essentially incorporeal.

Not having committed himself upon this last issue, Locke goes on to tackle the reidentification problem of personal-identity; but without ever addressing himself to the logically prior problem of how a person so defined is to be identified in the first place. As we have noticed again and again, this omission is a fundamental fault into which spokespersons for Platonic-Cartesian views of the nature of man traditionally fall; and it is no less a fault when, as in Locke, the component or function thought of as the real or essential person is not from the beginning defined as incorporeal.

In this context it is as interesting as it is unsurprising to notice that St Thomas Aquinas, who wanted to marry an Aristotelian with a Platonic conception of the human soul, appears to have managed never to address the identification problem: whether in either of the two Summae; or in his *Questions on the Soul*, where he begins: 'The first question that is asked about the soul is this: "Whether a human soul can be both a form and an entity. It seems that it cannot be both"'. He proceeds, of course, himself to contend that it can. Yet his entire procedure here is irredeemably wrongheaded and prejudicial. Thomas is, as it were, aspiring to be a kind of biologist: taking it that he has at his disposal a sufficiency of identified specimens; and can now proceed to investigate all their special characteristics. But these consequent investigations cannot sensibly begin until and unless the prior problem of identification has been satisfactorily solved. And that cannot be achieved until and unless we both have a concept of soul as an incorporeal substance (or, in the Thomist terminology, an entity; and have shown that this particular concept has application. Given this it would have become immediately obvious that a human soul must be an entity and not an Aristotelian form.

Two further points remain to be made about Locke's proceedings so far. First, however little credence we may put in the traveller's tale of a parrot person found in Brazil, we can scarcely accuse of gross conceptual impropriety those well-loved children's books in which brute characters are described as feeling and acting just like humans. (It is not for this reason that the most fanatic type of *Guardian*-reading 'progressive' would ban *Winnie-the-Pooh* and *The House at Pooh Corner*; but because Christopher Robin was bourgeois, and hence to be numbered in the ranks of the hated class enemy.) Yet to admit that some of the higher brutes could conceivably become capable of some of the feelings and behaviours characteristic of persons, and, hence that, if this conceptual possibility were actually realized, then they could properly be described as persons, is not to open the door to philosophically dangerous talk: either of the essential incorporeality of persons; or of the possibility of coming across incorporeal persons as a newly discovered variety. The brutes are, quite certainly, no less corporeal than us humans!

The second point concerns actuality rather than conceptual possibility. The enormously important and constantly underrated fact is that in the real world – the world with which all the natural languages have evolved to deal – the changes in personality which do normally occur are vastly less drastic and less abrupt than most of those envisaged by philosophers thinking up puzzle cases. The fun was started by Locke himself: 'I am apt enough to think I have in treating of this Subject made some Suppositions that will look strange to some Readers, and possibly they are so in themselves' ([1690] II.xxvii.27, p. 347).

They will, and they are. To the rational parrot in Brazil we have to add the Mayor of Quinborough, 'who was perswaded his had been the Soul of *Socrates*', and who 'as the Press has shewn, . . . wanted not Parts or Learning' (II.xxxii.13, p. 339). Two other conceivable cases Locke seems to have thought up without any stimulus from contemporary putative fact: that of 'the Prince' and 'the Cobler', whose souls simply swapped bodies (15, p. 340); and that of the 'two distinct incommunicable consciousnesses acting the same Body, the one constantly by Day, the other by Night' (23, p. 344). Incidentally, Locke's description of the first of these two suppositions may suggest, by its reference to a soul swap, that we have been offered: not only a description of a conceivable phenomenon; but also, and simultaneously, a sketch of an explanation for that conceivable phenomenon, were it actually to occur. But, until and unless we are provided with at least the embryo of an account of how such supposed hypothetical substances as souls might be first identified and then reidentified through time, that is not so.

Stimulated by advances in brain research and transplant surgery, there has in the philosophical literature since Flew 1951b been a fine efflorescence of fantasy. Consider, for example, the distressing case of Brownson, the product of what the fantasist was later to describe as 'a surgical blunder' of 'staggering proportions' (Shoemaker 1984, p. 78). The story went like this: 'Two men, a Mr Brown and a Mr Robinson, had been operated on for brain tumours, and brain extraction had been performed on both of them.' But the brains got put back into the wrong patients. One died, But the other, equipped now with what had been Robinson's brain, is given the compromising name of Brownson: 'Over a period of time he is observed to display all of the personality traits, mannerisms, likes and dislikes, and so on that had previously characterized Brown, and to act and talk in ways completely alien to the old Robinson' (Shoemaker 1963, pp. 23 and 24).

It is all very good, clean fun. Yet we ought never to forget, what almost always in the present context has been forgotten, that there is a categorical difference between fact and fiction. Our notions both of persons and of personal identity evolved in adaptation to the actual situations in which our ancestors found themselves; and they will no doubt continue to evolve if and in so far as our actual situations become in relevant ways drastically different. But considerations of how in future we either ideally should or in fact would alter these or other concepts, were we in truth confronted by this or that unquestionably conceivable yet way-out fantastic predicament, are simply not relevant to investigations of the present meanings either of the word 'person' or of the expression 'same person'. The crux, excellently put by one who wrongly believed himself to be disagreeing with me in so saying, is this: 'Difficult cases that would jeopardize the very notion of personal identity if they did arise do not therefore jeopardize it (let us never forget this) by their mere logical possibility even if they do not arise' (Geach 1977, p. 63; and compare Flew 1951b, especially pp. 66–7).

For the relatively smooth and modest personality changes which do in fact frequently occur, the vernacular already makes adequate provision. No one needs contest the claim that 'there are... changes in human beings such that we certainly feel like saying "That's not the same person"' (Hamlyn 1984, p. 213). But this secondary sense of the expression 'same person' is itself parasitical upon that primary sense in which personal identity is a matter of the continuing existence of an organism. We only say that our Harriet is quite a different person since she qualified as a nurse when we are quite sure that, in the primary sense, she is the same (Flew 1951b, p. 60).

Chapter Eight

Personal Identity:
(ii) Uniting Memories?

'I got my chin scraped. It hurts. It feels scraped. That way I know it's scraped. No I can't see it. I don't have to see it. It's my chin and I know whether its scraped or not. Maybe you want to make something of it.'

Raymond Chandler, *Farewell, My Lovely* (1949), p. 59

Suppose that some individual could suddenly become Emperor of China on condition...of forgetting what he had been, as though being born again, would it not amount to the same, in effect...as if the individual were annihilated, and an Emperor of China were the same instant created in his place?

G. W. Leibniz, *Reflections on Knowledge, Truth and Ideas* [1684], ch. XXXIV

In one of the two final, summing up contributions to *Personal Identity*, advertised as a 'Great Debate', it is written: 'We also agree in allowing as conceivable, and possible, various things (body-switching, disembodied existence, and the like) which many other philosophers have claimed to be inconceivable...' (Shoemaker 1984, p. 139). It is hard to decide which is more astonishing, the extent or the nature of this agreement. Certainly it is so extensive in relation to the disputed questions in this area as to prejudice the possibility of staging a satisfactorily confrontational debate. But for us the question which matters is how these two debaters contrive to come so easily to their common conclusions.

All such talk of body-switching and disembodied existence necessarily presupposes the conceivability of incorporeal switching substances. Consider, for instance, the plot of F. Anstey's *Vice-Versa* (1887), which as a play was at one time immensely popular in independent preparatory schools for boys. Fatly prosperous father and engagingly spirited schoolboy son are presented as exchanging total personalities; including all memories, skills and incapacities. But to describe and to attempt to explain this as an exchange of personalities, rather than as two total transformations occurring independently albeit simultaneously to two quite separate though biologically related individuals, presupposes the existence, and therefore the conceivability, of two potentially 'possessing' substances.

This presupposition is, of course, recognized by both of these debaters. In section 2 (iii) of chapter six we saw how in an earlier work one of them maintained that, although 'we may use bodily continuity to reach conclusions about personal identity', the truth is that it 'is something ultimate, not analysable in terms of bodily continuity . . .' (Swinburne 1977, pp. 109 and 110). The other also pointed out in an earlier work, quite correctly, that, 'if it follows from the definition of ''person'' that a person is a substance, it is surely self-contradictory to say that the identity of a person does not involve the identity of a substance' (Shoemaker 1963, p. 46). But neither has at any stage provided sense for the suggestion that the true subject of personal predicates is an *incorporeal* substance:

Beyond the wholly empty assurance that it is a metaphysical principle which guarantees continuing identity through time, or the argument that since we know that identity persists some such principle must hold in default of others, no content seems available for the doctrine. Its irrelevance . . . is due to its being merely an alleged identity-guaranteeing condition of which no independent characterization is forthcoming. (Penelhum 1970, p. 76)

What appears to have been the only attempt by either debater to meet this objection wholly fails to take its measure. The first move is to mistake the objector to be maintaining that the reason why the identity of bodiless persons cannot be accounted for in terms of memory claims is that in this case such claims could not be checked; and to suggest that sometimes perhaps they might be (Swinburne 1977, pp. 107–9). The truly devastating objection, however, not only in one particular and somewhat far-fetched case but in all others also, is one which, by all those tolerably familiar with the classical literature, is always attributed to Butler. (Apparently – see Behan – Butler was anticipated by an otherwise unknown John Sergeant.) The key sentence reads: 'And one should really think it self-evident, that consciousness of personal identity presupposes, and therefore cannot constitute personal identity; any more than knowledge, in any other case, can constitute truth, which it presupposes' (Butler 1896, I, p. 388).

The second, equally misguided move is to complain that Penelhum here fails to distinguish questions about meaning from questions about verifiability (Swinburne 1977, p. 110). But in fact Penelhum's claim, as we have just seen, precisely is a claim about the failure to provide not verifiability but meaning.

Both Shoemaker and Swinburne, like several of their greater predecessors, go wrong right from the start. For they rush on to questions about reidentification without first making sure that they have correct answers to the prior questions about identification (Teichman 1985). The difficulty of meeting this challenge while continuing to defend any kind of immaterialism did not escape the young Berkeley. For in the private notebooks of his twenties we find this prudential maxim: 'Mem. Carefully to omit defining of person, or making much mention of it' (1901, I, p. 41).

This advice Berkeley follows resolutely throughout his published works, with the significant exception of a passage in *Alciphron* where he challenges the minute philosophers, to 'untie the knots and answer the questions which may be raised even about human personal identity', before requiring a 'clear and distinct idea of *person* in relation to the Trinity' (VII.8; II, p. 334). Aficionados of our greatest master of controversial judo will compare this play with one in the *Principles*. There, realizing that he cannot provide for any natural knowledge of 'other minds', Berkeley, with characteristic verve, swings into the offensive: '. . .it is evident that God is known as certainly and immediately as any other kind or spirit whatsoever, distinct from ourselves. We may even assert that the existence of God is far more evidently perceived than the existence of men. . .' (I.147; I, p. 340). Indeed we may. We had better too, if we want to still murmurs about solipsistic implications (Flew 1978, ch. 10).

Insisting that people are a sort of spirits, Berkeley is in trouble about identification right from the beginning. Since there obviously cannot be a mental picture of anything incorporeal, it might seem that all spirits are destined to follow material substance into the dustbin of philosophical history. But in the second edition of the *Principles* there is, hopefully, a saving insertion: 'We may not, I think, strictly, be said to have an *idea* of an active being, or of an action; although we may be said to have a *notion* of them' (I.142, I, p. 338).

For some explanation of this new notion of notions we have to refer to the *Alciphron*, above all to the Wittgensteinian anticipations in Book VII. 14 (Flew 1974). There Berkeley argues, in a way which is as right as it was in his own day revolutionary, that terms may be significant 'not only although the ideas marked are not offered to the mind, but even although there should be no possibility of offering or exhibiting any such idea to the mind; for instance, the algebraic mark which denotes the root of a negative square, hath its use in logistic operations, although it be impossible to form an idea of any such quantity' (II, p. 344).

Both for the square root of minus one, and for all other such purely ideal denizens of the timeless world of pure mathematics, this is well and fine. But, as we saw in section 4 (iii) of chapter three, if we are seeking some warrant for harbouring Wisdom's 'logically unique expectation', then there simply is no substitute for the old-fashioned, this-worldly, in principle identifiability of actual individuals. By confusing dispositional with substantial interpretations of such words as 'minds' or 'souls' or 'selves', and in several other ways, we may be misled to think that proper provision has been made for this essential. Yet – for the incorporeal personal substances postulated by Swinburne, Shoemaker and so many others – identifiability as actual individuals is exactly what we have not got.

1   The implications of open texture

Consider those whose approach to the question how a person at time two is to be reidentified as the same person as at time one proceeds by way of some preliminary inquiry into the prior question how anything can be identified as a person in the first place. Even some of this happy few, this small band of pedestrian hardpersons, have failed to press on in the same robustly direct, simple-minded, feet-on-the-ground style. Instead of going on to inquire, for instance, what it is that courts are trying to discover when they ask whether the accused is the same person who did the deed, these people have allowed themselves to be sidetracked. Or else, even after recognizing the obvious and straightforward answers to such practical questions, they have not been content. They have longed for something more than physical continuity, something more or something different, something which would, at one and the same time: both provide, what in the nature of the case there cannot be, antecedently correct answers to all questions about personal identity in theoretically possible but never or scarcely ever actual puzzle cases; and make identity with the person who did the deed not merely a necessary but also the sufficient condition of warranted accountability.

These are matters which must be sorted out before we go on to discuss attempts by successors of Descartes to provide for the reidentification of persons misconceived as somehow incorporeal. That subsequent discussion, even when the whole project is seen to be doomed from the start, should still be sufficiently instructive. For such misconceived contributions can be – as we are told is said in the world of *Smiley's People* – turned round to serve as elements in the case for saying that it is impossible to construct a coherent concept of bodiless persons.

(i)   Bernard Williams began the first of his several papers on *Problems of the Self* by laying down what were for him two fundamentals:

There is a special problem about personal identity for two reasons. The first is self-consciousness – the fact that there seems to be a peculiar sense in which a man is conscious of his own identity . . . The second reason is that a question of personal identity is evidently not answered merely by deciding the identity of a certain physical body. (Williams 1973, p. 1)

It was, of course, entirely right to begin in this way by stressing the incomparable importance of both consciousness and self-consciousness. Both are essential to the possibility of rationality, agency, and all the other attributes largely or wholly peculiar to people. But to go on to say that 'a question of personal identity is evidently not answered merely by deciding the identity of a certain physical body' – suggesting that this is perhaps a consequence of the first fundamental – is, surely, just as evidently wrong?

For the truth is that in all ordinary and everyday cases – all the cases, that is, which actually do arise, as opposed to those merely conceivable cases so joyously excogitated by philosophers – physical continuity is not only the necessary but also, for all practical purposes, the sufficient condition of personal identity. Of course, whenever there has been this physical continuity, we harbour various confident expectations: that both the organism at time one will have possessed and the organism at time two will possess the various capacities and affections normal to persons; that there will have been a continuous development of personality from the earlier stage to the later; that the person at the later stage will be able to remember the earlier person's former deeds and sufferings as his own; and so on.

These and other, similar, confident expectations are in fact rarely if ever very drastically disappointed. If, however, falsifications did begin to be frequent, then these would no doubt require us to review our notions both of 'person' and of 'same person'; and perhaps, in consequence, to abandon our present practice of taking physical continuity between persons as the necessary and normally sufficient condition of personal identity. But to say this is precisely not to deny that our present practice is what it is, and is justified by the facts as they are.

Presumably the reason why Williams disagrees is that he is engaging with Butlerian 'strange perplexities'. These arise from conceivable cases – of a kind dear to philosophers – in which some person at time two would undoubtedly be the same as one particular predecessor at time one, in what was earlier distinguished as the primary sense of 'same person'; although the differences in verbal and non-verbal behaviour would be much greater than those normally compassed when someone is said – since his experiences in boarding school, boot camp, or you name it – to have become quite a different person, in the secondary sense of 'same person'. Thinking along these lines, Williams was perhaps bound to conclude that being the same person, in that primary sense, although perhaps necessary, could not be the sufficient condition of true personal identity.

His mistake here, if that was indeed how his mind worked, is extraordinarily common; indeed it has been almost universal. It consists in the misunderstanding and misuse of possible puzzle cases; cases which if they actually occurred and were thought likely to recur, would require us to make new decisions as to what in future correct verbal usage was to be. What is wrong is to assume that decisions, even the most rational decisions, about responses to purely hypothetical challenges, and usually challenges which we have no reason or less than no reason to expect to have to face in real life, must throw direct light upon the present meaning of the words concerned. These present meanings are determined not by hypothetical future but by actual present correct usage; while our ordinary language provides us with the concepts with which it does provide us because these were those which were evolved in and adapted to the worlds in which our ancestors lived – concepts most of which are more or less adequately adapted to dealing with most of the predicaments in which we find ourselves today.

Two supplementary comments may help: both to fix the main point in mind; and to explain why it has been so persistently neglected. The first revives the notion of 'open texture' (Waismann 1951). The term 'ship' is vague, since a whole spectrum of similarities stretches between things which are certainly ships, via the things which provoke linguistic hesitation, to the opposite extreme of undoubted boats. But, when a court has to decide whether, in a statute passed by one of the parliaments of Elizabeth I,

'ship' covers flying boats, then the difficulty arises: not so much
from the vagueness of the term (that would imply that the drafting
of the statute was bad and might have been improved); but from
what Friedrich Waismann would have described as *die Porosität
der Begriffe* [open texture]. Vagueness could have been removed
by prescribing that, within the meaning of the act, nothing under
so many tons was to count as a ship: 'To remove vagueness is
to outline the penumbra of a shadow. The line is there after we
have drawn it, and not before.' Certainly we can always prescribe
against vagueness. But to eliminate open texture would be impossible: requiring us, in advance and with total foresight, to rule
decisively upon every possible puzzle case.

The second supplementary comment refers to the reasons why
we are all inclined to share the confidence of those so sure that
there must be an account of personal identity capable of yielding
clearcut, antecedently true answers to all possible puzzle questions. Even those fully aware that many legal rulings about the
correct application of terms are really decisions about what in
future the law is to be, rather than unequivocally valid inferences
from preexistent statutory premises, remain reluctant to accept
that there are parallel possibilities with the term 'person' and the
expression 'same person'. It must be different with us, they want
to protest. For are we not people rather than mere things?

This reluctance is reinforced by a common conviction – based
upon the familiar fact that people do usually know a lot more about
their own pasts than they wish to reveal – that the individuals
themselves must always have the true answers. Surely, we muse,
he himself cannot fail to know whether he is the man who broke
the bank at Monte Carlo? Even if we cannot discover the answer,
even if he protests that he does not know, still we assume that
he must remember really, and merely be trying to deceive us.
For that is not the sort of thing anyone would forget. Insensate
sticks and stones are no doubt different. But surely people could
always tell, if only they would: 'Where-ever a Man finds what
he calls *himself*, there, I think, another may say is the same *Person*'
(Locke [1690] II.xxvii.26, p. 346)?

Of course this is all wrong. Amnesia and paramnesia are not
only logical possibilities but also actualities. Yet to break the

hold of the common conviction that it is not wrong, we need a truly apocalyptic puzzle case. So let us suppose, what is not merely conceivable but vividly picturable, that someone splits like an amoeba: developing first into connected Siamese twins; but shortly separating into a pair of monozygotic identicals. Suppose too that both are able accurately to recall everything that the original undivided person could remember. Then Locke would have to say that two obviously different people were both the same as that original one. Which is absurd.

This apocalyptic example was, so far as I know, first published in Flew 1951b. Certainly it was employed there to enforce exactly the same points as have been made again here. Perhaps the reason why those points have been taken so rarely and so incompletely is that those who have found a use for the example seem never to have refreshed their memories of the context of its first employment. Thus one writer attributes it to C. B. Martin, though Martin himself was to refer most generously to Flew 1951b (Williams 1956, p. 23; and contrast Martin 1959, p. 96) Another finds it in the *Blue Book*, though a quick check would have shown that the mention there of amoebas is not in connection with personal identity (Swinburne 1984, p. 35; and contrast Wittgenstein 1958, pp. 5 and 61ff.) When, twenty years later, some philosophers revived the example, along with the point which it was first introduced to enforce, the only one showing any awareness of anticipation by a much earlier predecessor showed it in a characteristically ungenerous and exploitative way: by first rejoicing to correct again a long since admitted and later removed error in that predecessor's earliest work; and by then, without any further or more direct acknowledgement of indebtedness, drawing from this borrowed example a similar moral – but again in his own characteristically and wearisomely complicated fashion. (David Wiggins in Rorty 1976, pp. 104–5 and 142ff; and contrast Hamlyn 1984, pp. 212–13.)

(ii) The short sentence from Locke quoted in the previous subsection comes from a paragraph in which he goes on to say that '*Person*. . .is a Forensick Term appropriating Actions and their Merit; and so belongs only to intelligent Agents capable of

a Law, and Happiness and Misery' ([1690] II.xxvii.26, p. 346).
This claim ties in with his insistence upon the importance, both
forward- and backward-looking, of his inquiries: 'In this *personal
Identity* is founded all the Right and Justice of Reward and Punishment; Happiness and Misery, being that, for which everyone is
concerned for *himself*. . .' (18, pp. 341–2).

Undoubtedly it is a mistake, and a mistake which often occurs,
to assume that an adequate account of personal identity must
make it the condition, not only necessary, but also sufficient,
of proper accountability. For there is an abundance of possible
extenuations or even of complete excuses. It would, however,
be at least a less obvious mistake, and perhaps no mistake
at all, to argue that we would and/or should accept it as a
condition both necessary and sufficient of that peculiarly in-
tense concern which it is normal, even if perhaps deplorable,
for human beings to feel about their own individual futures.
Certainly it is to me not obvious either that I in fact would,
or that I rationally should, agree with Leibniz about the worth-
lessness of an offer, upon the terms proposed, of the Chinese
Empire.

2 Memory proposed as the uniting principle

We have already, more than once, indicated the reason why
personal identity is not to be analysed in terms of memory powers:
even the most promising of answers to the question 'How do you
know?' cannot but be disqualified as responses to the question
'What do you know?' Given that previous, repeated emphasis upon
the ultimate impossibility, what needs to be said now is that,
immediately, and to anyone misguidedly resolved to eschew
considerations of corporeal continuity, an attempt at an analysis
on these lines offers the least unhopeful prospect. So true is this
that, in the two centuries and more since Bishop Butler's magisterial refutation of Locke, there have always been, whether in
ignorance or in defiance of that refutation, some philosophers
eager to try again (Grice 1941 and Quinton 1962; and contrast
Flew 1963b).

(i) The solution which Locke himself proposed is this: 'That with which the *consciousness* of this present thinking thing can join it self, makes the same *Person*, and is one *self* with it, and with nothing else; and so attributes to it *self*, and owns all the Actions of that thing, as its own, as far as that consciousness reaches, and no farther; as everyone who reflects will perceive' ([1690] II.xxvii.17, p. 341). Locke is not wholly consistent in his usage of the term 'consciousness'. But we shall not go far wrong if we take it as covering, in the present context, memory and something more: what we are, in this understanding, conscious of doing is what we can remember doing in the past; plus what we are or can be aware of doing now.

In offering this account Locke was encouraged by two beliefs: both that personal identity with the original agent, and that being able to remember doing whatever it was, are both necessary and sufficient conditions of proper accountability. The second of these became a cause of embarrassment, and of capitulation as a philosopher.

He first wishes to forbid the occurrence of paramnesia – seeming to remember doing what in fact you did not do: 'one intellectual substance may not have represented to it, as done by it self, what it never did, and was perhaps done by some other Agent...' Locke, apparently, does not realize that, were his analysis correct, there would be no such possibility. But he does recognize that the employment of his proposed criterion might lead to great injustices. So he calls up his theological reserves:

And that it never is so, will by us, till we have clearer views of the Nature of thinking Substances, by best resolv'd in the Goodness of God, who as far as the happiness or Misery of any of his sensible Creatures is concerned in it, will not by a fatal Error of theirs transfer from one to another, that consciousness, which draws Reward or Punishment with it. (II.xxvii.13, p. 338)

Modernized and abbreviated, Locke's central contention is that a person at time two is the same as a predecessor person at time one if an only if that person at time two can remember his doing or feeling what that predecessor did or felt at time one. Two of the terms in this account are relevantly ambiguous. 'Can' may be: either 'can' as a matter of fact, hereafter rendered as 'can (factual)'; or it may be 'can' without self-contradiction be said to, hereafter rendered as 'can (logical)'. There is also a more subtle ambiguity in 'remember'. This is best brought out by symbolic examples. 'He knows p' entails p is true, whereas 'He said that he knew p, and he was not lying' does not entail p is true. Similarly, 'He remembers p' entails p is true; whereas 'He said that he remembered p, and he was not lying' does not entail p is true. For, just as it is both possible and common to be honestly mistaken in a claim to know something, so it is possible and common to be honestly mistaken in making a claim to remember something. When someone challenges a knowledge claim or a memory claim he is not necessarily, or even usually, challenging the claimant's integrity. He is much more likely to be questioning the truth of the proposition said to be known or remembered. If the proposition is in fact false, then this is sufficient to defeat the claim really to know or truly to remember. (Another possibility, mentioned only to be dismissed as here irrelevant, is that the critic is either challenging the adequacy of the grounds available to support the knowledge claim or challenging the implicit claim to have been in the past in a position which qualifies the claimant to be remembering now.) We have, therefore, to distinguish between genuine remembering, which necessarily involves the truth of the proposition said to be remembered, and making honest memory claims, which does not.

Let us now ring the changes on these alternative interpretations of 'can' and 'remember'.

First, taking 'can' as logical and 'remember' as entailing the truth of what is remembered, Locke's definition becomes a necessary truth, albeit a futile necessary truth. On this interpretation, what we have is of course not open to attack on the ground that it is too exclusive or too inclusive. It is, simply, an otiose, only too true truism.

Second, taking 'remember' in the same way as referring to genuine remembering and 'can' as can (factual), Locke's definition is open to two objections. First, it excludes too much. Often, and rightly, we want to say that we must have done something or other, although we cannot for the life of us remember doing it. Second, there is The Paradox of the Gallant Officer. This objection seems to have been put first, in a monochrome version, by Berkeley in *Alciphron* (VII.8). Later it was remade in full and glorious colour, in the *Essays on the Intellectual Powers of Man*: 'Suppose a brave officer to have been flogged when a boy at school, for robbing an orchard, to have taken a standard from the enemy in his first campaign, and also to have been made a general in advanced life' (Reid [1785] III.6, p. 213). Then, if the young officer could remember the flogging, and the general could remember taking the standard but not being flogged as a boy, on Locke's principles we should have to say that the general both is and is not the same person as the orchard robber. He is not the same, because he cannot now remember the robbery, and yet he is the same, because he is the same as the young officer who was in turn the same as the boy thief.

The third possibility is to take 'can' as can (logical) and 'remember' as involving only the making of an honest memory claim. The objection to this is that it will let too much in. This point, too, was, it seems, first made by Berkeley in the private *Philosophical Commentaries*:

Wherein consists identity of person? Not in actual consciousness; for then I'm not the same person I was this day twelve-month, but while I think of what I then did. Not in potential; for then all persons may be the same, for aught we know... Two sorts of potential consciousness – natural and praeternatural. In the last section but one I mean the latter. (1901, I, pp. 72–3)

It is our present point which Berkeley is making since his praeternatural potential consciousness is obviously equivalent to ability to remember, in the present interpretations of 'can' and 'remember'.

The fourth possible combination, that of 'can' as can (factual) with 'remember' as involving only the making of an honest memory claim, yields an interpretation open to all three objections made against the thesis in interpretations two and three. First, it leaves too much out, ignoring amnesia. Second, it lets too much in, ignoring paramnesia. Third, it is internally inconsistent, being exposed to The Paradox of the Gallant Officer.

(ii) If once we have made ourselves familiar with Butler's magisterial refutation — that memory may reveal but cannot constitute personal identity — then the exhaustive ringing of the changes in the previous subsection may have seemed superfluous. But that curt dismissal has not in fact sufficed to spare us later and more elaborate attempts to conscript either memory or some wider form of consciousness of identity to serve as the crucial binding element in what used to be called a Serial Theory of the Self. So a more thorough treatment was needed, first of Locke and then of some modern manoeuvres within the same tradition.

Perhaps the most heroic of these was the assertion that 'it cannot be a part of what I seem to remember about this experience that 1, the person who now seems to remember it, am the person who had this experience' (Parfit 1971, p. 15). If this were true then Butler's objection would, of course, collapse: if memory does not reveal, then maybe it could constitute personal identity. Notwithstanding that reviewers have hailed the same author's later book as 'something close to a work of genius' (Parfit 1986, dustjacket), we must not accept this earlier revelation simply on his own sheer authority. On the contrary: it is plumb obvious that, when I remember doing this or feeling that, what I remember precisely is that I am the person who was doing this or was feeling that.

Certainly, there could be circumstances in which 'I should cease to assume that my apparent memories must be about my own experiences' (Parfit 1971, p. 16). If these circumstances were to arise, and if these apparent memories contained correct information about the experiences of others, then parapsychologists would no doubt want to speak of retrospective telepathy, or R psi-gamma (Flew 1987). But, once again, it is wrong and may be ruinous to treat the logically possible as if it were actual, and to construe current terms as if their meaning either already had been, or now imperatively has to be, adjusted to the realization of such conceptual possibilities. An example of this bad practice comes in the summing up of that 'Great Debate' on *Personal Identity*: 'I now prefer to define "remember" in such a way as to allow the logical possibility of someone veridically remembering, from the inside, actions and experiences other than his own' (Shoemaker 1984, p. 148).

A less heroic but more helpful observation is that memory, like perception, 'is a causal notion; it is a necessary condition of a person's remembering a past event that his apparent memory of that event should be caused, in an appropriate way, by that event itself' (1984, p. 83). The truth of this observation does nothing to undermine Butler's objection to Locke's explication of the meaning of the expression 'same person'. But it is relevant to some other sorts of story which have been offered as 'theories of personal identity' (Perry 1975, p. 67). If, for instance, we are trying to explain why we are properly held responsible for what we did, and why most of us are so much more concerned about our own individual futures than about those of others, then our findings are bound to embrace, apart from a general reference to evolutionary biology, some emphasis upon the more particular fact that all humans – indeed all living creatures – are in a peculiarly privileged position for influencing what their own individual futures are to be.

Suppose now that we do take constant care to distinguish the different questions to which 'theories of personal identity' could offer possible answers. Then we might find it interesting and worthwhile to explore in various other directions. We might, for instance, develop some rejigged notion of a personality such that it would become proper to speak of the same, even numerically the same personality 'possessing' or 'inhabiting' what were, in our ordinary understanding, different persons. Although it would, even in this new interpretation of 'personality', remain as nonsensical to speak of subsistent personalities as it is to talk of bodiless persons, still we could, just because such personalities would be categorically different from persons, require that a disposition to make certain memory claims be a necessary condition of personality identity.

Much of what Locke himself said might be reconstructed into a suggestion: not of what is meant by 'same person'; but of what might be meant by 'same personality'. Unlike persons, such personalities could significantly be said to swap their corporeal habitations; although, not being substances (or 'subsistent things'), they could not exist between tenancies in any Limbo. Unlike persons too, personalities could be allowed to go out of existence and yet return in a second beginning: the personality of the Mayor of Quinborough might have been the same as that of Socrates; yet the two persons neither were nor could have been.

A lot of what is today contributed to anthologies with titles like *Personal Identity* or *The Identities of Persons* should be seen as similarly reconstructionist, rather than as underlabouring, conservative, philosophical analysis. Certainly it would be altogether absurd to think of holding personalities responsible, rather than persons. As a minimum first step to their becoming qualified to be properly held to be responsible it would surely be necessary somehow to endow earlier states of the same personality with some power to affect their successors.

3 Personality and personhood

A little, but only a very little, needs to be said about the characteristics which are in fact peculiar to people; and hence about what is involved when we personify some creature which is not a member of the species Homo sapiens, or of any of the other species recognized as kinds of man. This very little can most conveniently stand here as an addendum to the treatment of personal identity. We shall not attempt more than a brief review of the suggestions made by Daniel Dennett.

The first theme in his order is 'that persons are *rational* beings' (1976, p. 177). Bertrand Russell, and others, having made so much cheap fun of the Aristotelian definition of 'man' as 'the rational animal', we need to gloss this: emphasizing that the opposite of 'rational' here is not 'irrational' but 'non-rational'; and explaining that only a being rational in this primary sense could properly be charged with irrationality. We shall also do well to distinguish two aspects of such rationality, which can perhaps be separated only in thought: reasoning, as thinking what follows from or is incompatible with what; and having, and being able to offer, reasons for acting in this way rather than that. This beginning, with its stress on rationality rather than on any kind of consciousness, is Platonic rather than Cartesian.

'The *second* theme,' says Dennett, 'is that persons are beings to which states of consciousness are attributed, or to which psychological or mental or *Intentional predicates*, are ascribed' (p. 177). This second theme is as Cartesian as the first was Platonic. The formulation suggests, what Dennett himself would certainly deny, that the attribution of 'psychological or mental or *Intentional predicates*' just is the attribution of particular sorts of states of consciousness. The truth is, of course, that the relevant states of consciousness are at most one essential, while behaviour and dispositions to behave are also necessary (Ryle 1949). Dennett notices at once how Strawson takes up this theme: he 'identifies the concept of a person as "the concept of a type of entity such that *both* predicates ascribing states of consciousness *and* predicates ascribing corporeal characteristics" are applicable' (p. 177).

Dennett continues: 'The *third* theme is that whether something counts as a person depends in some way on an *attitude taken* toward it, a *stance adopted* with respect to it' (p. 177). Although he goes on to list me among those who have expressed 'Variations on this theme', I cannot persuade myself that I was ever guilty on this score. Certainly I would not now want to go beyond entertaining the suggestion that human infants could not grow into people if they were never treated as such. I further submit that any contention that the status of person can be arbitrarily granted or refused, and is not sufficiently legitimated by the satisfaction of various purely factual requirements, must carry morally disturbing implications.

Dennett himself links his fourth theme with his third. But this is unnecessary. The connection with the fifth is much less easily broken. His '*fourth* theme is that the object to which this personal stance is taken must be capable of *reciprocating* in some way'. The fifth is 'that persons must be capable of *verbal communication*'. The sixth, and last, is 'that persons are distinguishable from other entities by being *conscious* in some special way . . .

Sometimes this is identified as *self*-consciousness of one sort or another' (p. 178). It was, presumably, the having of this rather than the having of sense-data and bodily sensations, which at the end of the day Descartes really wanted to pick out as the one essential characteristic distinguishing men from both the brutes and unoccupied human bodily machines (Cottingham 1978a and b).

The only omission which occurs to me – a replacement for the original third theme – is agency. In effect I brought this in under Dennett's first head, by construing his '*rational* beings' as rational *agents*. But those two aspects of rationality do deserve separate consideration. And, in the consideration of rational agency, we do need to bring out: both that such agents can, and cannot but, make choices; and that it is of them always true to say that, in the most fundamental sense, they could have done other than they did (Flew and Vesey 1987).

Chapter Nine

Substances, Stuff and Consciousness

If there were not this internal illumination, then the Universe would be a mere rubbish heap.

> Albert Einstein, in conversation with Herbert Feigl, recorded in K. R. Popper and J. C. Eccles, *The Self and Its Brain* (1977)

How it is that anything so remarkable as a state of consciousness comes about as the result of irritating nervous tissue, is just as unaccountable as the appearance of the Djinn when Aladdin rubbed his lamp, or any other ultimate fact of nature.

> T. H. Huxley, *Elementary Physiology* (1915), Lesson 8

Descartes set up for his successors two kinds of problem about consciousness and stuff. Given that the subjects both of pure consciousness and of the various psychological, mental or intentional predicates which, if they do not necessarily presuppose, normally involve the occurrence of particular forms thereof, are supposed to be essentially, or at any rate potentially, incorporeal substances, the first of these problems is to explain how such putative entities are first to be identified and then reidentified through time. The second is to explain how the two equally familiar and yet, it would seem, unbridgeably separate worlds of consciousness and stuff can be and are related. It is this second problem which has, traditionally, been dignified with the name Problem of Mind and Matter. And it is to this that psychophysical parallelism, two-way interactionism, epiphenomenalism and – since World War II – The Mind/Brain Identity Theory have been offered as answers, or sorts of answers.

(At this point all old-timers of British philosophy will pause to recall, with an affectionate smile, C. D. Broad's *The Mind and its Place in Nature* (1925), and especially the list of seventeen different theories, several of which were to be put down as self-contradictory and/or advocated only by Oxford men.)

1 No-ownership, Serial Theories of the Self

Until Hume all the successors of Descartes seem to have thought of all sorts of consciousness as always owned or had or to be predicated of (either essentially or potentially incorporeal) spiritual substances; although, as we have seen, even when the questions of identification and reidentification were seen as problems, no one had any satisfactory answers.

Hume, even 'the ungullible Hume', failed to challenge the fundamental Cartesian contentions; and, in consequence, failed to find the answer to the problem of personal identity in the continuous existence of an organism which is itself the only possible subject of all such 'mental' predicates. Instead he preferred a bold, not to say reckless, approach: first denying that we do or could have experience of an incorporeal subject of our own consciousness; and then suggesting that we, or at any rate our 'selves', simply consist in a series of collections of unowned 'perceptions of the mind'; distinguished by Hume into the two categories of 'ideas and impressions'. Such no-ownership, Serial Theories of the Self have, even in our century, been attempted by Russell and by Ayer, by Grice and by Quinton. They should, nevertheless, be recognized as reductions to absurdity of the presuppositions which require their development.

(i) Hume's discussion 'Of personal identity' is found in the *Treatise*, and it is a topic to which he never returns. Some forty pages before he begins to address himself to the problem, Hume, equating 'these ideas of self and person', gives notice that, on this assumption, 'there is no question in philosophy more abstruse than that concerning identity, and the nature of the uniting principle, which constitutes a person'. This observation is made in the course of inquiring 'how far we are *ourselves* the objects of our senses'. The question is alleged to be difficult, presumably because Hume believes that 'in common life 'tis evident these ideas of self and person are never very fix'd nor determinate'. He concludes: ''Tis absurd, therefore, to imagine the senses can ever distinguish between ourselves and external objects' (I.iv.2, pp. 189–9).

It is an index of the extent to which Hume's Cartesian assumptions have been shared that so few critics appear to have recognized that it is, rather, his own abrupt and negative conclusion which is the absurdity. For a start, it is only a sort of philosophers and perhaps psychologists who ever speak of selves or The Self; although everybody, whether specialist or layperson, employs, and possesses a sufficiently clear understanding of, the reflexive personal pronouns – 'himself', 'herself', 'myself', 'yourself', and so on (Flew 1950a).

Then, next, there can, in that everyday understanding, be no question but that 'we *are* ourselves the objects of our senses'; that it is not absurd but obvious that the senses can 'distinguish between ourselves and external objects'. For to each of us individually both all other people and every non-human thing are all equally 'external objects'; while a provident Nature has supplied us all with skins by which we are, in a very sensible and determinate fashion, separated from all the rest of the furniture of the Universe. What was there to stop Hume gazing at his own notoriously bulky person, and thus discerning once more the altogether familiar differences between himself and both the domestic equipment and the rest of the company? (Since they have almost always been overlooked, these elementary and excruciatingly obvious objections do need to be laboured.)

When he actually begins his discussion 'Of personal identity' Hume sets off in fine style: 'There are some philosophers, who imagine that we are every moment intimately conscious of what we call our SELF; that we feel its existence and its continuance in existence; and are certain, beyond the evidence of a demonstration, both of its perfect identity and simplicity' (I. iv.6, p. 251). If once we allow that persons are incorporeal, and in view of the fact that none but a rival philosopher would be so prissily affected as to speak of 'our SELF' as opposed to ourselves, then we have to concede to Hume a win in the first round, on a knockout. For what we may indeed by intimately conscious of when we are aware of ourselves as subjects of experience — in either interpretation of that Janus-faced term (Flew 1971, VI 6) — is one particular specimen of that kind of creatures of flesh and blood to which we all in fact belong; rather than any incorporeal substance which might or might not be causing us to have some impression from which an idea of self could be derived.

Hume goes on to triumph in successfully not finding that impression. In the next sentence he draws out a consequence which, if that were possible, must make the forlorn hope of finding the uniting principle of such a 'self or person' even more forlorn: 'When my perceptions are remov'd for any time, as by sound sleep; so long am I insensible of *myself*, and may truly be said not to exist.' This Cartesian conclusion was one which, as we have seen, had revolted the common sense of Locke, who harried it through ten sections of the *Essay* (II. i. 10-19). Heedless of those objections, Hume considers he has established that - 'the rest of mankind ... are nothing but a bundle or collection of different perceptions, which succeed each other with an inconceivable rapidity, and are in a perpetual flux and movement' (I.iv.6, p. 252).

(ii) It is notorious that, in an Appendix written as he was preparing Book III for the press, Hume disowned his positive account of personal identity: 'upon a more strict review . . . I find myself involv'd in such a labyrinth, that . . . I neither know how to correct my former opinions, nor how to render them consistent' (p. 633). There is, therefore, no need for us to follow him down that blind alley. (But see Flew 1986a, ch. 6). What does demand attention is the never repudiated thesis that his 'perceptions of the mind', his 'ideas and impressions', are, in our sense, substances. For this is a thesis which, though totally wrong, has been assumed or even outright asserted by an apostolic succession of often formidably able neo-Humians. In *The Analysis of Mind*, for instance, we read:

> We say: 'I think so-and-so' and this word 'I' suggests that thinking is the act of a person. . . It is supposed that thoughts cannot just come and go, but need a person to think them. Now of course it is true that thoughts can be collected in bundles, so that one bundle is my thoughts, another is your thoughts. . . It would be better to say 'it thinks in me', like 'it rains here', or better still, 'there is a thought in me'. (Russell 1921, p. 18)

Again, in a set of Gifford Lectures delivered recently in St Andrews we were: both told that 'it is quite legitimate to ask whether an experience of such and such a sort is one that I am having'; and invited to 'explain how thoughts and images are brought together with percepts to form a single series of experiences' (Ayer 1973, pp. 117 and 115).

In a section 'Of the immateriality of the soul' immediately preceding 'Of personal identity', Hume challenges 'certain philosophers', unnamed, about 'the material or immaterial substances, in which they suppose our perceptions to inhere' (I.iv.5, p. 232). It would, he urges, be an evasion to reply 'that the definition of a substance is *something which may exist by itself*; and that this definition ought to satisfy us' (p. 233).

Hume himself responds by maintaining 'that this definition agrees to every thing, that can possibly be conceiv'd'. Appealing to some of his fundamental principles, he concludes,

> that since all our perceptions are different from each other, and from every thing else in the universe, they are also distinct and separable, and may be consider'd as separately existent, and may exist separately, and have no need of any thing else to support their existence. They are, therefore, substances as far as this definition explains a substance. (p. 233)

If indeed it does follow from those fundamental principles that sense-data can significantly be said to exist unsensed by anybody, or that a throbbing pain could intelligibly be asserted to occur loose and separate, and not as the pain suffered by a particular person, then that constitutes a sufficient reason first to rethink and then, at least in part, to reject those principles.

Hume himself, in one of his 'epic inconsistencies' (Passmore 1952, p. 94 and *passim*), had earlier volunteered 'to explain that *distinction of reason*, which is so much talk'd of, and is so little understood, in the schools' (I.i.7, p. 24). Whether or not we are prepared to admit that explanation, Hume's admission of such distinctions of reason itself concedes that sometimes what we can separately conceive could not be conceived as existing separately. We can, for instance, perfectly well discuss a shape without mentioning either a size or any object so shaped. We can also review sorts of sense-data without stating either that these must be had, or who has them. Yet from none of this can we validly deduce the false conclusion that both shapes and sense-data are, in the appropriate sense, substances.

(iii) Once the truth of the previous paragraph is grasped we see what the problem is: not to 'explain how thoughts and images are brought together with percepts to form a single series of experiences'; but rather to discover how anyone ever came to assume that they could have been got 'loose and separate' in the first place. Furthermore, as was so dryly remarked of Alexander Bain, who maintained 'that the mind is a collection. Has he ever thought who collects Mr Bain?' (Bradley 1876, p. 36n).

Certainly, Hume is continually referring to the activities of what – all his denials notwithstanding – sounds painfully similar to one of the agent spirits of Berkeley. *Quasi veritate coactus* [as if compelled by the truth] Hume refers in his every statement to 'we', or to 'the mind', or to 'the imagination', as allegedly reviewing, or passing over, or reflecting upon those successive 'perceptions of the mind' of which minds or selves are alleged wholly to consist. Thus he infers 'that identity is nothing really belonging to these different perceptions, and uniting them together; but is merely a quality, which we attribute to them, because of the union of their ideas in the imagination when we reflect on them' (I.iv.6, p. 260).

Compare also: 'the transition of the mind from one object to another' (p. 254); 'the passage of the thought . . .' (p. 256); 'the mind...feels an easy passage from the surveying its condition in one moment to the viewing of it in another' (p. 256); 'there is, however, another artifice, by which we may induce the imagination to advance a step further' (p. 257); and so on.

2   Direct knowledge of bodiless continuity?

Suppose that, in accordance with Hume's official view, and with that of so many others, we take it that Humian 'perceptions of the mind' can significantly be said to occur unowned; that they are all a sort of substances, rather than affections thereof. Suppose too that a memory claim just is such a Humian idea or Humian impression. Then it may seem that in the occurrence of an experience of the relevant kind there is direct, unevidenced knowledge of the earlier occurrence of another experience belonging to an earlier collection in one of those series of collections of all sorts of experiences which selves are supposed to be. (If all this is felt to be – as indeed it is – intolerably far-fetched, suppositious and at best only doubtfully intelligible; then it should be recognized as the fairyland into which anyone is got who, by refusing to press the question how minds or souls are to be identified at all, if not as those of particular flesh and blood people, takes leave of the concrete and corporeal.)

Consider now how one of our own contemporaries would present such a thesis about our memories of our earlier doings and feelings. In what is by the almost geological standards of philosophers a recent book, *Self-knowledge and Self-identity*, the author maintains 'that a major source of the problem of personal identity is the fact that persons make what appear to be identity statements about themselves, namely memory statements about their own past histories, without having or needing the sort of evidence we use in making identity judgements about persons other than ourselves' (Shoemaker 1963, p. 123).

This contention is unexceptionable; or, rather, it is unexceptionable so long as we are permitted to construe it as a polite pointing to what has in fact misled so many to follow false trails. On the same page the passage continues: 'Since one can make such statements about oneself, and know them to be true, without first knowing the facts which would justify an assertion about the identity of one's body, it appears that bodily identity cannot be the criterion of personal identity and is at best only contingently correlated with it.'

Certainly it is true that, when I remember my doing or feeling something, I do not employ bodily criteria in order to determine that I am indeed the same person as did or felt whatever it was. I need to refer to that sort of evidence only if there is some reason to doubt the correctness of my original memory claim. But as the same author later concludes, the reason why I do not, at least in the first instance, appeal to bodily criteria is not that I am relying on non-bodily criteria instead. It is that my claim is to direct memory knowledge; which, precisely in as much as it is direct, precludes the employment of any criteria at all (1963, p. 207).

The temptation is to conclude: that, because such direct memory knowledge of personal identity employs no corporeal criteria, it must therefore be direct knowledge of the identity of something incorporeal; that, because the how-do-we-know appears not to refer to the bodily, therefore the what-it-is-that-we-know must be correspondingly bodiless. However, even if claims about personal identity were not – as they are – claims about the identity of creatures which are essentially corporeal; nevertheless it would still not follow, from the fact that no body was actually mentioned, that the existence of a body was not entailed or presupposed. We need to recall in the present context what was said in section 1 above about the possibilities of distinguishing in thought what could not be separated in reality; as well as the account provided much earlier of the Masked Man Fallacy.

3   The traditional mind–body problem

As set by Descartes this problem has been that of determining what are the relations between mind and body, conceived as consciousness and stuff. With the possible exception of epiphenomenalism the main traditional answers appear to make, or at any rate not to contest, the assumption that we are dealing with two sorts of separable substances, either or both of which might sensibly if not truly be said to be the causally sufficient conditions of changes in the other. Thus, while the two-way interactionist maintains that the two sorts actually do interact causally, those who, like the Occasionalists, thought that causal transactions between such radically different substances must be inconceivable went on to advocate some sort of psychophysical parallelism. Thus, although the physiological disturbance can neither cause nor be caused by the bodily sensation, still there may be a parallelism; in which a Preestablishing Harmonizer makes each not the cause but the occasion of the other, a parallelism in which all kinds of 'perceptions of the mind' could apparently occur without being the affections of any organism. By contrast the epiphenomenalist asserts that consciousness is an epiphenomenon – always an effect but never an independently isolable sufficient cause. (It is only, in Curt Ducasse's mischievous analogy, the halo on the saint!)

(i) Given the traditional two-substance frame of thought, then, of course two-way interactionism must be the favourite to beat. It was, therefore entirely fitting when a chapter entitled 'The Traditional Problem of Body and Mind' started from the question: 'Why should so many distinguished men, who have studied the subject, have denied the apparently obvious fact of Two-sided Interaction?' (Broad 1925, p. 97). This question becomes the more urgent once we realize that some equally 'distinguished men, who have studied the subject' have continued to insist that it is indeed an obvious fact.

For instance: in his book *The Self and Immortality* Professor H. D. Lewis declares that his aim is 'to break down the materialist presuppositions of much contemporary thought. . . by what we find to be the case in ordinary experience. . . ' (1973, p. 204). But he in fact reaches the desired Cartesian conclusions by taking it that an exclusively Cartesian interpretation of various familiar ongoings is itself an essential part of our ordinary experience of those ongoings. Thus, for instance, he says: 'If my wife calls and I go downstairs, this is because I understand that dinner is ready, etc.; and surely my understanding counts, short of treating all purposive activity as some curious sort of reflex action' (p. 64).

Certainly Lewis, and Mrs Lewis, and everyone else, knows that his understanding her call is on this sort of occasion a causally necessary condition of his going downstairs. But this familiar fact simply does not begin to show that two substances, conscious mind and non-conscious matter, have been causally interacting. Nothing has been done, therefore, to prepare for the question on the following page: 'But why should we expect that or suppose that proper scientific study of the brain at its own level precludes the recognition that the impact of our thoughts upon it alters considerably what would have happened otherwise?'

To argue on these Lewis lines does nothing to foreclose on the possibility that consciousness can be significantly predicated only of living organisms. To insist that such 'ordinary experience' as that of my hands moving because I decide to move them, or of my suffering agonies because a weight is crushing my leg, proves 'a close interaction of mind and body', is not at all to show that in these cases extended physical entities are engaged in causal transactions with something 'of a radically different nature from extended or physical reality'. Absolutely nothing has been said to rebut the studiously simple-minded contention that the deciding agent and the suffering patient are one and the same flesh and blood person. Nor has anything whatever been said to show that either pure moments of consciousness unalloyed with anything material, or incorporeal subjects of consciousness, either have been, or could be, isolated as independent causal factors.

Let us now come at the same question from a marginally different direction. Suppose we wanted to show that, for a particular organism to behave in a particular way, it was necessary for that organism, immediately before – as Skinner would put it – it emitted that behaviour, to have been affected by one certain state of consciousness. Then it would be necessary to show that it is by no means sufficient for that organism to have been in whatever (public) purely physiological condition normally precedes the emission of that behaviour. For it would also be necessary to show that that behaviour was not in fact emitted unless being in that particular (public) purely physiological condition always involved being in that particular (private) 'one certain state of consciousness'. But of course no one has any notion of how to isolate an organism's state of consciousness from the general physiological condition of whatever organism is – shall we say? – subject to that state. We face here one token of a too rarely noticed type. As M. Levin in his recent *Metaphysics and the Mind–Body Problem* opined: 'Nobody knows how to get a leg to be raised in the way it is when it is raised intentionally without getting someone to intend to raise his leg' (1979, p. 84).

We must, however, point out that there are ways in which an organism's being in some state of consciousness at one time can be a causally necessary condition of certain later cognitive achievements. But to say this is not to say that we can, after all, isolate 'loose and separate' moments of consciousness; and identify these as independently operating causal factors. So this present observation requires at most a reformulation rather than the total rejection of epiphenomenalism.

The point to observe is that, just as it cannot be true to say that I could at that time see my philosopher's table unless its presence before my eyes was a causally necessary condition of my having the appropriate sense-data (Flew 1971, p. 355), so I cannot truly be said to know now that I had those sensory experiences, or indeed any others, unless my having them was itself a causally necessary condition of my later believing that I did have them. This observation is, however, no help to anyone wanting to prove the causal efficacy of consciousness. For all the behaviour which would normally justify the verdict that the behaver believed this proposition might conceivably be emitted without the propositions being true.

(ii) Before passing on to consider a second weakness in the traditional treatments, it is worth saying a word or two about evolutionary implications. These were very vigorously discussed in the nineteenth century. In 1895, for instance, Bradley published in *Mind*, against the epiphenomenalism of T. H. Huxley and W. K. Clifford, a characteristically crushing paper 'On the Supposed Uselessness of the Soul'. In our own day too Sir Karl Popper and others have sought 'The Biological Function of Conscious and of Intelligent Activity'. Thus, in *The Self and Its Brain*, Popper writes: 'Much of our purposeful behaviour (and presumably of the purposeful behaviour of animals) happens without the intervention of consciousness. What, then are the biological achievements that are helped by consciousness?' (Popper and Eccles 1977, p. 125).

There are two dangers here. First, we may be misled to insist that consciousness *must* have a function; that there *must* be achievements which it helps to make possible. But Neo-Darwinian theory affords no guarantee that everything which survives will have positive survival value. It does no more than make it overwhelmingly likely that anything possessing a balance of survival disvalue will be eliminated (Flew 1984). Writing in 1895, Bradley was, therefore, wrong, after speaking of 'Darwinian teleology', to go on: 'Everything which on a certain scale persists must be taken as useful. It was not made to be useful, but, if not useful, it would by now have been unmade' (1935, I, p. 343).

Second, the fact which we have just now noted, that we cannot isolate a condition of consciousness from the more purely material state of the organism characterized by that condition, makes it impossible to specify any particular piece of pure behaviour which, unless preceded or accompanied by consciousness, causally could not occur. Certainly, as we have just seen, we could not truly say that she knew she had had some experience in the past unless her having had it was a causally necessary condition of her now believing that she had had it. But she could, of course, at least on one particular occasion, emit all the verbal and non-verbal behaviours appropriate to a person sincerely claiming to know that she had had that experience, without her having had that experience.

What is called the Problem of Other Minds thus starts from the observation that there is no (public) behaviour, described in strictly behaviouristic (necessarily public) terms, the occurrence of which strictly entails that the behaver is being affected by some form of (necessarily private) consciousness; although certainly we should (ought to), and most of us would (in fact), hesitate to apply 'psychological or mental or *Intentional*' terms to any creature which we believed to be, despite all appearances, deeply unconscious. In a nutshell: the crux is that consciousness, as such, offers no purchase to the forces of natural selection.

It is also possible here, as a further fruitful aside, to indicate the fatal flaw preventing the consummation of the once seemingly so promising project of analytical behaviourism (Ryle 1949). It seemed promising because most of the reference of most of these terms in fact is to behaviour and to dispositions to behave; rather than to the occurrence of members of peculiar classes of 'perceptions of the mind'. To say, for instance, that she has understood her arithmetic lesson is to say that she has become able to do sums of the sort therein presented; rather than that she experienced then a once-for-all moment of inner illumination, a revelatory and self-guaranteeing 'click' of comprehension. Nevertheless the primary and non-Freudian application of all such terms presupposes that the people to whom they are applied are indeed conscious; that they are, that is, neither fast asleep nor deeply anaesthetized. This is indeed a large part of what is involved in treating people as people or – if you must – as souls; although – *pace* Dennett and others – treating people as people is not immediately even a part-cause of their actually being the creatures which should be so treated.

(iii) There is a second kind of confusion which afflicts discussions of the traditional mind–body problem. Claims about mental characteristics are confused with claims about mental substances: those wanting to deny the latter assume that they have also to deny the former; while those convinced of the reality of the latter mistake it that this is sufficiently evidenced by the manifest and inescapably familiar realities of the former. This second kind of conclusion is then often further confounded by a failure to distinguish three varieties of behaviourism. Of these the first is the analytical behaviourism, mentioned earlier. The analytical behaviourist maintains that the meanings of psychological notions can be completely analysed in terms of behaviour and of dispositions to behave, without any reference to the consciousness of the behaver.

By the way: this is a convenient occasion to make parenthetical mention of a not previously recorded fact. Some ten years after the first publication of *The Concept of Mind* I suggested, in one of a series of second-thoughts reviews for the BBC World

Service, that Ryle should have presented this book as an attempt to discover how far the programme of analytical behaviourism could be pressed, an attempt made by a philosopher perfectly well aware that it could not possibly be completed, but also very conscious that the behavioural element in the meanings of psychological terms had been, in the mainstream Cartesian tradition, grotesquely neglected. A frank admission of this impossibility, right from the beginning, would have spared us, for instance, the shifty shufflings of Ryle's chapter VIII, designed to hush up the scandalous occurrence of mental imagery. Instead this all had to be sorted out by Annis Flew in her 'Images, Supposing and Imagining', published in *Philosophy* for July 1953. (For a similar sorting of a later article misled by Ryle, compare Flew 1956b.) Already in 1951 or 1952, when he was first shown that particular criticism of the chapter on 'Imagination', he accepted it all; and when later I showed him the script of that broadcast talk he fully agreed with its general line too.

Returning to distinguishing between varieties of behaviourism, the two others are methodological and metaphysical. The methodological behaviourist does not as such deny either the reality of consciousness or the truth that psychological terms often refer to that reality. His contention is that introspective inquiries are profitless, and that the future of psychology as a science lies in the study of behaviour. But metaphysical behaviourism is, or would be, the denial of any reality to consciousness. It is hard to believe that there ever have been, or could be, any sincere and wholehearted believers. But certainly J. B. Watson himself did from time to time assert metaphysical behaviourism, presumably because he mistakenly thought that it is somehow presupposed by methodological behaviourism; the doctrine to which he really was – not without good reason – sincerely and wholeheartedly committed.

The confusions noticed in the present subsection are of very long standing. Over sixty years ago Gifford Lectures on *The Idea of Immortality* observed 'that the motive prompting the assertion of the soul's substantiality was the wish to deny that the conscious life is...merely an attribute...of body, body alone possessing the kind of permanent reality usually associated with the term substance' (Pringle-Pattison 1922, p. 169; and, for a confession from the psychologist William McDougall that that motive is in its turn prompted by the desire to open the door to doctrines of a future life, compare Pringle-Pattison, p. 74).

The same confusions and, in one of the two authors, the same motivations, can be seen in *The Self and Its Brain*. Thus Popper, after disclaiming both any desire for immortality and any intention to discuss the substantial souls which immortality might be thought to presuppose, goes straight on to argue, explicitly against Hume, 'that *selves exist*' (Popper and Eccles 1977, p. 101; and compare p. 146). Eccles, however, is less inhibited. He asks 'What happens in death?' To this 'ultimate question' he answers: 'Then all cerebral activity ceases permanently. The self-conscious mind that has had an autonomous existence. . . now finds that the brain that it has scanned. . . is no longer giving any messages at all' (p. 372).

Because, and it would seem only because, he cannot but accept the reality of all those familiar phenomena of or involving consciousness, Popper too insists upon some form of inter-actionism. But, 'even if one cannot say anything about the nature of the interaction, substances are the kind of thing between which it makes sense to speak of interaction' (Hamlyn 1984, p. 165). We could scarcely ask for a bolder Cartesian manifesto than Popper here provides: 'I said in Oxford in 1950 that I believe in the ghost in the machine. That is to say, I think that the self in a sense plays on the brain, as a pianist plays on a piano or as a driver plays on the controls of a car' (Popper and Eccles 1977, pp. 494–5).

4 The Mind/Brain Identity Theory

Section 3 showed how easy and how common it is to pass, by an immediate yet illicit inference, from a recognition of the reality of consciousness and an insistence upon its importance, to the conclusion that this either itself is, or exclusively characterizes, a peculiar sort of substance; and that necessarily disembodiable and presumably incorporeal. It appears that, on the opposite side, those who are concerned to reject that conclusion, but perhaps fail to appreciate the fallacy in this supporting argument, find it correspondingly easy to bring themselves to assert that in fact there is, despite all appearances, no such thing as consciousness. I quote one of several similar statements made by highpowered scientific contributors to a conference on Artificial Intelligence, a conference held in 1986 in New Haven, Connecticut: 'The real problem is that people who ask "could a machine be conscious?" think that they are. They think they have a pipeline to what is happening in their minds. That's not true.'

Speaking at the same conference Professor H. D. Lewis, who, as we saw earlier, is inclined to see some sort of two-way inter-actionism as given in everyone's everyday experience, said, of recent scientific work on the central nervous system, that 'such advances...do nothing to bridge the gap between mental and physical processes or to explain why one should influence the other in the ways we find to be the case...In the last resort we have to make do with what in fact we find to be the case.' What our brain scientists can hope to discover, and what in fact they have been and are discovering, is what kinds of consciousness people will suffer or enjoy when this or that is going on in their brains. So, for anyone who has realized what is wrong with interactionism, all such discoveries would seem to support an epiphenomenalist conclusion: states of consciousness are effects of the brain states which accompany them.

It appears that Lewis himself, along with many others, is going to remain dissatisfied no matter how close and how numerous are the correlations which the brain scientists discover between particular sorts of state of the central nervous system and particular kinds of state of consciousness. It might be salutary if, before pushing any further, we were all to ask ourselves: 'What would the desired further and more fundamental explanation look like?'; or, 'Could someone please suggest even a false explanation, to show exactly what the question is to which an answer is desired?'

Before we finally drop the topic of epiphenomenalism, we have to mention two further objections. First, it might seem that the epiphenomenalist is committed to maintaining that – since consciousness in and by itself, and except as characterizing the organism which is conscious, is causally impotent – therefore it cannot be important. But the contrary conclusion is, manifestly, presupposed by all judgements of value and, therefore, of intrinsic importance. (What could conceivably be more important for scandalously self-centred Flew than the question whether his future consciousness is going to be agreeable or agonizing?)

Second, it might also seem – to many it has seemed – that even the most cautious epiphenomenalist is committed to maintaining that there can be no room for any explanation of human behaviour as consequent upon the desires and decisions of the agents so acting. But this again is a conclusion in part deriving from a false assumption. The false assumption this time is that a sufficient account of what it is for people to decide to act, and actually to act, can be given while referring only to modifications of and changes in their consciousness. Even if *The Concept of Mind* showed nothing else, it certainly showed that that will not do. (It would be as wrong, surely, as to give accounts making no reference to consciousness at all?)

(i) There are anticipations of the Mind/Brain Identity Theory in Hobbes, Spinoza and Schopenhauer; and no doubt also elsewhere (Flew 1964; and compare Presley 1967 and Borst 1970). But it is only since World War II that it has been elaborately developed and extensively discussed. It is, surely, best understood as an attempt to improve upon epiphenomenalism (Beloff 1965, p. 36); and there is no doubt but that its chief champions have been philosophers who, in an earlier generation, would have been equally enthusiastic for epiphenomenalism. In its simplest and most persuasive form the Mind/Brain Identity thesis is that for a person to be in such and such a state of consciousness just is for that person's central nervous system to be in some corresponding physical state. The analogies most usually offered are the identity of lightning with an electrical discharge; and, less happily, that of the Morning Star with the Evening Star. All are agreed that philosophical underlabouring can do no more here than remove some of the rubbish which lies in the way to knowledge. The Identity Thesis will be established, if it ever is, only by scientific advances showing that every sort of state of consciousness does in fact have its corresponding, and hence at least arguably identical, state of the central nervous system.

It is rather less easy to discover why this theory is thought to be an advance on epiphenomenalism, or even why that view is not now acceptable. One reason sometimes offered is that the Identity Thesis restores causal sufficiency to states of consciousness: 'This is so because raw-feel terms are then precisely in those loci of the nomological net where science puts (what dualistic parallelism regards as) their neural correlates' (Feigl 1958, p. 475). The moral drawn is that – *pace* Beloff (1965, p. 47) – if the state of consciousness is identical with the physiological state, then both must fully share the same causal properties.

Another reason, much more frequently and much more forcefully pressed, is that states of consciousness, on an epiphenomenalist view, either are or are connected with other things by 'nomological danglers'. They are not, as has been incorrectly asserted, defined as constituting 'exceptions to physical laws' (Hamlyn 1984, p. 178). J. J. C. Smart explains his usage in a much reprinted article on 'Sensations and Brain Processes'. States of consciousness, he complains, 'do seem to be the one sort of thing left outside the physicalist picture, and for various reasons I just cannot believe that this can be so' (1959). Were this the case then 'Such sensations would be "nomological danglers", to use Feigl's expression.' This statement is glossed in a footnote: 'Feigl uses the expression . . . for the laws whereby the entities dangle. I have used the expression to refer to the dangling entities themselves' (1959, pp. 53–4 and 54).

In its simplest and most persuasive form, however, the Identity Thesis does not dispose of this perceived scandal. For, so long as the reality of both terms in the alleged identity is still conceded, the truth of all the putative equations remains an unexplained brute fact; a residual fact of a kind about which Smart is not alone in feeling uneasy.

(ii) Smart of course was not himself prepared to leave it at that. Instead he went on to develop what 'it would be tempting to call . . . the Australian Heresy, since its main support appears to be among Australian philosophers'; but what its 'principal spokesmen' have christened "Central-State Materialism"' (Beloff 1965, p. 38). Happily there is no need for us to go deeply into a formidably complicated business. It is here sufficient to grasp the fundamental truth that the entire enterprise is an attempt to realize the project of physicalism.

The word 'physicalism' is often defined, as it is in the *Fontana Dictionary of Modern Thought*, to mean 'The theory that all significant empirical statements can be formulated as statements referring to *publicly* observable physical objects' (Bullock and Stalybrass 1977, p. 472). In the present context it is obvious that this admits far too much. It is necessary to add that the characteristics attributed to those '*publicly* observable physical objects' must also themselves be '*publicly* observable'. This addition rules out what it was always intended to rule out; namely, statements attributing (always private) states of consciousness to those always '*publicly* observable physical objects' – people.

Once we realize what the coveted implications of physicalism are, then it becomes obvious why there can be no profit for us in entering into the elaborations and complications of Central-State Materialism. For their only relevant effect must be either to deny or to conceal precisely those manifest and inescapable truths denied by metaphysical and not researched by methodological behaviourism. It is, therefore, nothing more nor less than grotesque to pretend that we either could or should aim to produce a science which is at one and the same time not only completely comprehensive but also committed to either denying or ignoring a most manifest fact – the fact that the Universe contains creatures of the kind we are, creatures capable both of consciousness and self-consciousness, both of suffering and of understanding.

There is, nevertheless, one possible consolation for the physicalist. For, although the class of significant empirical statements is not, as he or she would wish, restricted to those referring only to '*publicly* observable physical objects' and attributing '*publicly* observable' characteristics thereto; nevertheless it does remain profoundly true that statements about someone's private consciousness can be significant only insofar as the meanings of their terms are explicable by reference to the publicly and interpersonally observable. (See, for instance, Flew 1961, ch. II)

Chapter Ten

The Significance
of Parapsychology

Does a man of sense run after every silly tale of hobgoblins
or fairies, and canvass particularly the evidence? I never
knew anyone, that examined and deliberated about nonsense
who did not believe it before the end of his enquiries.
> David Hume to the Rev. Hugh Blair, *Letters* (1932)

When we took up seriously the obscure and perplexing
investigation which we call *Psychical Research*, we were
mainly moved to do so by the profound and painful division
and conflict, as regards the nature and destiny of the human
soul, which we found in the thought of our age...it appeared
to us that there was an important body of evidence – tending
prima facie to establish the independence of soul or spirit –
which modern science had simply left on one side...evidence
tending to throw light on the question of the action of mind
either apart from the body or otherwise than through the
known bodily organs.
> Henry Sidgwick, in his second Presidential Address to the (British)
> Society for Psychical Research, *Proceedings*, V, pp. 272–3

As is made clear by the second of the two epigraph quotations
above, the venerable Founding Fathers of psychical research were
distressed by the clash between Platonic–Cartesian and Aristotelian
conceptions of the nature of man. They saw contemporary
advances in the mainstream sciences as providing ever more and
stronger confirmation of the Aristotelian alternative. The only

hope of recruiting similar support for their own preferred Platonic –Cartesian option lay in the subject-matter of the new science which they themselves were engaged in founding. At the time of his first election as president of the SPR Sidgwick was Knightsbridge professor in the University of Cambridge, and had already published one of the classics of moral philosophy.

(He had earlier resigned his Fellowship of Trinity College because he could not in honesty make the then required religious commitment: a sacrificial stand which some will compare most favourably with the very different behaviour of so many of our contemporary ecclesiastics who, apparently having lost whatever Christian and other-wordly faith they may once have had, now prefer to propagate some secular, this-wordly and always more or less socialist substitute, while nevertheless continuing to act under the auspicies of still nominally Christian organizations. See for instance, Flew 1986b.)

In his third Presidential Address, later printed in the same volume of the *Proceedings of the SPR*, Sidgwick went so far as to say: 'There is not one of us who would not feel ten times more interest in proving the action of intelligences other than those of living men, than in proving communication of human minds in an abnormal way' (V, p. 401; and compare Flew 1987, Introduction).

Two further facts about the Founding Fathers need to be emphasized. First, the original list of Members and Associates of the SPR included a remarkable number of names which in many different fields either already were or were about to become distinguished: A. J. Balfour, for instance, a future Prime Minister, William Bateson the geneticist, Leslie Stephen, John Ruskin, the Reverend C. L. Dodgson (better known as Lewis Carroll), and many others.

Second, all these Members and Associates were seemingly of impeccable high Victorian respectability. It has nevertheless since emerged, largely through the vastly painstaking researches of one independent scholar, Trevor Hall – that such appearances were sometimes deceptive. The most important of these cases was perhaps that of Sir William Crookes, FRS. As much as a century later his involvement with Florence Cook was still cited, thanks to his authentic achievements as a physicist, as providing authoritative endorsement of the genuineness of her performances as a physical medium. The truth is that Crookes was a crook, and the medium was his mistress (Hall 1962 and 1985, and compare Hall 1964, 1965 and 1984).

1 The evidential situation

In a philosophical rather than a scientific exercise we are not required to solve the problem of what, if anything, psychical research has definitively established. As the slick contrast has it: Scientists ask 'What in fact happens, and why?'; whereas philosophers worry the question, 'So what?' A few words do nevertheless need to be said, if only to indicate that there have been developments since the days when such leading philosophers as C. D. Broad and H. H. Price kept the whole field under constant review. Although, since their time, a few successors have continued to show some interest, no one of comparable standing has been so continuously concerned as those two were (Broad 1962 and Price 1972). There are also methodologically important theoretical problems about the character of the evidence which we must solve if we are to allow that parapsychology – a new name for psychical research – really does possess its own peculiar and authentic subject-matter.

(i) In a great series of Gifford Lectures, delivered now nearly fifty years ago in Edinburgh, a most distinguished student of the central nrevous system remarked that the names given to the vitamins were, at first, 'non-committal in order that scientific ignorance should not be cloaked. Under fuller knowledge they are already being christened properly and chemically. Vitamin C is ascorbic acid...' (Sherrington 1940, p. 96). It is as significant as it is depressing that only after World War II did parapsychologists at last accept the soundness of this policy. Unfortunately they, unlike the biochemists, have not achieved that 'fuller knowledge' which would make possible the replacement of a scrupulously non-prejudicial by a more informative terminology.

The putative phenomena of parapsychology are thus now most properly distinguished into two kinds: psi-gamma; and psi-kappa. The expression 'psi-gamma', or the Greek letters so pronounced, cover what used to be called telepathy, clairvoyance and paranormal precognition; or, comprehensively, extra-sensory perception (ESP). The suggestion that the equally misleading temporal descriptions 'retrocognitive', 'simultaneous' and 'precognitive' should be replaced by the Latin letters R, S and P has not, however, been widely adopted. The expression 'psi-kappa', composed of the initial Greek letters in the Greek words for, respectively, 'mind', and 'movement' replaces the single word 'psychokinesis' (PK), meaning movement by the mind. The main merit of this modest and austere vocabulary is that it carries no false suggestion that we know how the various supposed cognitive and kinetic results are achieved. The truth of course is that 'psi-gamma' and 'psi-kappa' are so defined as altogether to preclude the employment of any – or at any rate of any ordinary and known – means or mechanism.

In *Philosophy* for 1944 Broad hailed the work of Dr S. G. Soal as the 'Experimental Establishment of Telepathic Precognition'. At that time very few of those who were familiar with these experiments, and with much other work published by the SPR, would have been prepared outright to deny the reality of all the putative psi-phenomena; although Soal himself was as incredulous as anyone about the psi-kappa claims coming from Professor J. B. Rhine's laboratory in Durham, North Carolina. The situation has, however, changed; as, in over forty years, might have been expected.

The most dramatic development has been the decisive discrediting of all Soal's own work. Since the publication of Volume LVI of the *Proceedings of the SPR*, which began in 1974, no one denies that Soal himself was faking the scores of his two star subjects, Gloria Stewart and Basil Shackleton. In view of the impact which those experiments had had this revelation would in any circumstances have been disturbing. But what should be seen as making it still more significant is another negative fact. Although, since Soal and his later disillusioned colleague K. M. Goldney published their 'Experiments in Precognitive Telepathy' in Volume XLVII of the *Proceedings of the SPR*, much more work has been done in parapsychology than ever before, we still appear to be as far away as ever from any repeatable demonstration of the reality of any psi-phenomenon. No one is able to offer us any algorithm such that, if only we are careful to do this and this and this, in such and such scrupulously controlled conditions, then the occurrence of some psi-phenomenon is guaranteed.

In the absence of any strictly repeatable demonstration, questions about the competence and honesty of particular researchers become crucially important. The issues are made the more intractable by the fact that the phenomena sought are negatively defined. No movements and no ostensibly cognitive achivements can qualify as psi-phenomena save in so far as they are compassed without any, or at least without any normally recognized, means or mechanism. In the opening words of one especially thoughtful Presidential Address, 'The field. . . must be unique in one respect at least: no other discipline, so far as I know, has its subject matter demarcated by exclusively negative criteria. A phenomenon is, by definition, paranormal if and only if it contravenes some well founded assumption of science' (Beloff 1963, p. 101).

(ii) The words 'well founded assumption of science' were carefully chosen. For what the occurrence of psi-phenomena is incompatible with is not, as has so often been suggested, some named law of fairly elementary physics – Ohm's Law or Boyle's Law or the like. What such occurrences would indeed be incompatible with is what Broad, in an article entitled 'The Relevance of Psychical Research to Philosophy', published in *Philosophy* for 1949, picked out as certain 'basic limiting principles' (BLPs). His account of these was both unnecessarily abstract and pervasively Cartesian. To appreciate both what he meant and how right he was we need: both to think of these BLPs in concrete terms as prescientific, wordly-wise principles which guide ordinary people to rule out certain conceivables as practically impossible; and to appreciate that and why it was seriously misleading for Broad to intrude his own Cartesian assumptions into his presentation of various particular BLPs.

Suppose, first, that there has been yet another leak of high security material from government offices in London, Bonn or Washington. Then no one, or almost no one, ever suggests that hostile agents, operating from afar, might have 'read' either the secret documents themselves or the private minds of their writers by the meansless means of clairvoyance or telepathy. That is ruled out as something which we have overwhelmingly strong experiential reason to dismiss as physically impossible. Again, after the Chernobyl disaster, neither the Soviet authorities – understandably desperate to find someone else to blame for what this second time could not be concealed – nor even their most fanatical friends in the USA and allied countries, ever suggested that the whole affair was the result of a PK operation mounted by the CIA. (For a skilful, painstaking and courageous deployment of the evidence for the occurrence of that first catastrophe, see Zhores Medvedev 1979.)

Notice, second, that by introducing those Cartesian assumptions Broad to some extent, and against his own best natural scientific inclinations, contrived to 'naturalize' PK; to make this strange suggestion seem like something to which we have abundant analogies in our most immediate and familiar experience. Thus Broad's formulation of his BLP No. 2 reads: 'It is impossible for an event in a person's mind to produce *directly* any change in the material world *except certain changes in his own brain* [later emphasis added].'

Certainly the acceptance of these assumptions does do a lot to make the occurrence of psi-kappa, and perhaps of psi-gamma also, seem more probable. Certainly too it has helped to conceal another significant negative fact – the lack of even the most rudimentary theory offering some promise of development into a comprehensive explanation of all the various sorts of psi-phenomena; if indeed they do actually occur, and if it really is their actual occurrence which we have to explain. Even a very rudimentary theory would do something to 'naturalize' psi-phenomena, and hence to probabilify their actual occurrence (Flew 1980).

Since, as we have just seen, we have the best of experiential reasons for believing that psi-phenomena are practically impossible; and since, as we have also seen, we lack any theoretical reason for holding that their occurrence possesses even a modest degree of antecedent probability; nothing but that repeatable demonstration which – never forget – we have not got, should be accepted as decisive proof that the phenomena are real; and hence that our BLPs have got to be, at the very least, radically revised. Any people discouraged by this discovery that it remains reasonable to doubt whether any genuine parapsychological phenomena do really occur may console themselves with the thought that, whatever the ultimate verdict on parapsychology, even people with extremely high thresholds for belief recognize important differences between the claims of the parapsychologists and most of the other allegations falling within the scope of the originally Buffalo-based, but now effectively international, Committee for the Scientific Investigation of the Claims of the Paranormal. It is quite different, that is to say, from the factitious, but richly profitable mysteries of the Bermuda Triangle and the Chariots of the Gods, from astrological prediction, from the extraterrestrial identification of Unidentified Flying Objects, or from most of the other affairs dealt with so faithfully in that committee's useful and entertaining journal *The Skeptical Inquirer*.

In this one exceptional case we may allow – indeed we surely must – that there is more than sufficient warrant for continuing the investigations; although, until and unless the holy grail of true repeatability is discovered, every report of psi-phenomena – including all reports of experimental work – must be treated as a miracle story. Since, as we should have learnt from Hume's notorious treatment of historical evidence for the miraculous, the canons of critical history require us to apply to all the detritus of the past all that we either know, or believe that we know, of what is possible and impossible, probable and improbable, we cannot, at best, reach about any such story any verdict stronger than a cautious, and appropriately Scottish, 'Not proven' (Flew 1961, ch. VIII; 1966, ch. 7; and 1986a, ch. 5).

2 Platonic–Cartesian assumptions in parapsychology

In 1900 the Classical scholar F. W. H. Myers, one of the founders of the SPR, described its goal as being to prove 'the preamble of all religions', by making it possible to say to theologians and philosophers: 'thus we demonstrate that a spiritual world exists, a world of independent and abiding realities, not a mere ''ephiphenomenon'' or transitory effect of the material world.' Indeed, in the fifteenth volume of the *Proceedings* he went on to express his conviction that this goal had already been achieved, saying: 'our method has revealed to us a hidden world within us, and . . . this hidden world within has revealed to us an invisible world without' (p. 117). In this, it should by now be obvious, Myers was far too optimistic.

Those on the other side of the argument are apt to agree that to admit the reality of the psi-phenomena would be to open the door to some sort of non-material world. Thus in *Body and Mind* Keith Campbell allows that 'if even a single example of. . . paranormal phenomena is genuine, Central-State Materialism is false' (1970, pp. 91–2). Similarly D. M. Armstrong gives in *A Materialist Theory of the Mind* several possible ways of 'explaining away' the data of parapsychology, and then remarks that 'if these ways of escape prove unsatisfactory, Central-State Materialism cannot be the whole truth about the mind' (1968, p. 364). But here, as we shall soon see, Campbell and Armstrong both capitulate far too readily.

(i) In the earlier days, before anyone had begun to talk of parapsychology, most psychical research was the study of what were thought of as the phenomena of Spiritualism: mainly mediumship in the context of a séance room; but also the unpremeditated 'seeing' of apparitions. The temptation, to which almost all the researchers seem to have succumbed, was to accept any paranormal phenomena which they believed that they had discovered at, as it were, their own self-evaluation. If the medium came up with information which could not have been normally available to her, then the presumption was that this information came, as in her trance she herself said that it did, from some discarnate spirit. If there was any genuine physical mediumship, or if there were any genuine poltergeistic phenomena, then these too must be the work of boisterous spirits. (The very word 'poltergeist' means, literally, a blustering or boisterous spirit!)

Thanks mainly to a landmark article by E. R. Dodds, who eventually became Regius Professor of Greek in the University of Oxford, it is now generally recognized that any attempt to explain such phenomena in Platonic–Cartesian terms must be, at least in the present state of our ignorance, grossly uneconomical. Even suppose that for the moment we ignore the difficulty, amounting perhaps to the impossibility, of providing means for identifying and reidentifying these postulated spiritual substances; a difficulty or impossibility which seems never to have been so much as mentioned in the literature until at least twenty years after the first publication of Dodds (Flew 1953, ch. VII). Then the offence to soundly Ockhamist principles of scientific economy lies in the fact that, whereas any Spiritualist account, after first postulating a sort of discarnate spiritual substances, then has to endow these with powers of psi-gamma and psi-kappa, its entirely this-worldly, non-Spiritualist rival attibutes whatever psi-powers do have to be admitted exclusively to the various people found to be involved.

It is, surely, obvious that if any such discarnate spiritual substance is either to acquire and transmit information or to move any material object, then these achievements can only be effected by the employment of its psi-powers? It is perhaps less obvious, and certainly less often remarked, that we should no more attribute memory to a being without the storage capacity of a central nervous system than perception to one without sense-organs. So, if such a being is to produce information about its own past learnings, doings and feelings, then it will have to bring this about by an exercise of paranormal retrocognition, or R psi-gamma.

The only yet still only partial exception to all this would appear to be if it temporarily ceased to be discarnate, and became incarnate as the spirit 'possessing' some medium. Once we realize how much must be missing from a discarnate spiritual substance we shall be rather readier to entertain Broad's unenthusiastic suggestion about psychic factors. The idea was that 'minds' might be 'a compound of two factors, neither of which separately has the characteristic properties of a mind, just as salt is a compound of two substances neither of which by itself has the characteristic properties of salt' (Broad 1925, p. 535).

Another merit of theorizing along these lines is that it takes account of the notorious fact that the intellectual powers of what are supposed to be the returned spirits of the eminent appear to have declined to the more pedestrian level of those possessed by the medium out of working hours. Such theorizing also fits the equally notorious fact that, although there is much talk of spiritual growth and of learning, 'in the glorious Summerland', what is actually communicated indicates not so much improvement as degeneration; and again, certainly, never any advance upon the ratiocinative capabilities of the medium.

When all the positive things have been said we still have to insist that a readiness momentarily to entertain this psychic factor suggestion cannot be allowed to conceal the difficulty, amounting perhaps to the impossibility, of developing any coherent and applicable notion of incorporeal spiritual substance. This objection applies both to psychic factors and to incompletely personal Thomist souls, just as strongly as to their fullgrown Platonic or Cartesian paradigms.

Finally, before proceeding to the next subsection, we have to mention the Gordon Davis case. Before his interests shifted to quantitative experimental tests for psi-gamma, Soal did a lot of work with mediums. He alleged: that in one session with Mrs Blanche Cooper a communicator calling himself Gordon Davis appeared; that 'he' spoke in what Soal remembered as exactly the Davis voice; that at the time Soal believed Davis to be dead; but that later it emerged that Davis was alive and practising as an estate agent in Southend. Dodds and others have wanted to make something of this story in the present context (Geach 1969, p. 15). But in a soon to be published book Melvin Harris shows that in this earlier work too Soal falsified the records.

(ii) The leading figure in the movement towards and the development of experimental, laboratory work in what has, under that leadership, come to be called parapsychology, was the American J. B. Rhine. ('Parapsychology' means, etymologically, beside psychology; and the term expresses the aspiration that these studies will eventually be accepted and incorporated into mainstream psychology.) Although it seems that Rhine himself never either worked with mediums, or manifested any great interest in the question of survival, he certainly did, especially in such best-selling popular books as *The Reach of the Mind* (1948) and *New Frontiers of the Mind* (1937), express his conviction that the reality of ESP and PK must constitute a knockdown proof for a Platonic –Cartesian view of the nature of man.

Yet in this, surely, Rhine was mistaken? For all the laboratory work which he reported so picturesquely, in terms of the doings of minds and of their transactions with matter, would be more calmly and more economically described as the performances of the various people serving as experimental subjects. We say that we are confronted with an ostensible case of psi-gamma: if a subject is told to guess the values of a series of concealed cards; and if, when his guesses are scored up against the targets, we find that the subject has scored significantly above mean chance expectation. We would say that we had seen a demonstration of psi-kappa if we had seen that some subject was able, without any direct or indirect contact, to move something about at will. Certainly there is no need to make any reference to any supposed spiritual substance in the description of such phenomena, and absolutely no warrant for so doing.

Picturesque expression is, no doubt, appropriate in books written for a wide, lay public. But unfortunately Rhine – like so many others both before and after – misconstrues the logic of this 'mind' terminology. What that means is this. When, sententiously, we talk of the triumph of Mind over Matter, such impressive expressions can always be replaced, with a loss of pomposity but a gain in precision, by workaday state-ments about how people do the most amazing things in spite of all handicaps of disease, disability, and poverty. But picturesque idioms must not be taken literally. To do so is to misunderstand their logic.

This is what Rhine and others seem to have done. Taking the word 'mind' to refer to some object, to some substance which could significantly be said to exist separately, he proceeds to assume that minds and brains can thus significantly be said to interact. He then tries to interpret his results in terms of this inter-action. Not surprisingly it is found to be mysterious: 'Science cannot explain what the human mind really is and how it works with the brain' (Rhine 1948, p. 7).

Again, Rhine complains that the student 'finds...in modern psychology...very little on the mind as a distinct reality. Instead he studies "behaviour" and its relations to brain fields and pathways' (1948, p. 9). But this does not convict psychologists of shirking the study of the mind: studying certain human capacities, feelings, and performances is what is meant by studying the mind. Mind talk is an alternative description of the same phenomena: it does not help to explain those phenomena; nor does it record the occurrence of further phenomena. Rhine starts a chapter entitled 'The Reach of the Mind in Space' by remarking: 'Experiences suggesting that the mind can transcend space are plentiful.' He continues: 'The spontaneous awareness of distant events, of which no knowledge could be acquired through recognized channels, is reported fairly frequently.' He then describes ESP work in which subjects scored significantly when widely separated from the target cards. But these phenomena are not *evidence for* further ghost phenomena taking place, as it were, offstage. They are part of what is *meant by* this talk of 'the reach of the mind in space' (1948, ch. 5).

Furthermore, Rhine complains that among psychologists 'even the word "mind" as used by the layman, meaning something different from the brain, is no longer in good standing' (1948, p. 9). At this point, if not long before, we should recall that Rhine had been a devoted pupil of William McDougall, a leading spokesman for an animistic (substance) account of the mind. Rhine in fact began his work in parapsychology with hopes and expectations parallel to those with which Margaret Mead first approached Samoa (Freeman 1983). In both cases pupils were confident that they would be able to produce a decisive vindication of the most controversial claims of their respective gurus.

Rhine and others have often claimed that psi-phenomena are, or would be, non-physical; and that, in these phenomena, we can see that the powers of the mind transcend the powers recognized by physics. It is, presumably, an uncharacteristically defeatist acceptance of these claims which has misled Campbell and Armstrong to concede that, if they had to admit the reality of psi-phenomena, then it would be all up with Central-State Materialism. Of course, if that thesis really does require us to deny the reality of consciousness, then it ought to have been all up with it right from the start. But psi-phenomena are, or would be, non-physical only in a very artificial and temporary sense; namely, that there would have to be yet another revolution in physics before they could all be comfortably accommodated.

The case of psi-gamma is more complicated than that of psi-kappa. For here what, apparently, is transmitted and received is information. But information is certainly no sort of substance. In the transmission of information, unlike in the transmission of material goods, the receiver's gain is not necessarily made at the sender's corresponding loss. Since psi-gamma would be, by definition, a kind of information transfer achieved either altogether without means or at least without any normal or already known means, this leaves the physicist with no urgent and immediate cause for concern. No doubt he would, if he were persuaded of the reality of psi-gamma, wish to seek some previously unknown physical means by which the information transfers are effected. But if information transfer as such were all there was to it, then failure would not be unduly upsetting.

The immediate and urgent cause for physical concern, however, is at the same time the reason why the Central-State Materialist has no need to worry. Certainly information as such is no sort of substance. But it is only in substances that it can, so to speak, manifest itself, that it can actually exist; or, perhaps we should say, more weakly, subsist. So, if there is to be any point at all in talk of psi-gamma as involving information transfers, as opposed to the occurrence of merely coincidental correlations between the information somehow embodied in both the 'sender' and the 'receiver'; then the reception must involve some changes in the recipient, changes which are not fully accountable in terms of the previous state of that recipient.

Certainly any such changes would fall unequivocally within the scope of physical science. Certainly too their occurrence could present the physicists with a very baffling and even perhaps wholly intractable problem. But the reason why such changes would be the business of physics precisely is that these recipients are creatures of flesh and blood. The changes occurring within these creatures are, therefore, material changes. As for the practically unbelievable phenomenon of psi-kappa, the theoretical case is perfectly clear. What could be more material than a woman demonstrating her psychokinetic powers, or more physical than the force exercised in this demonstration? (For more, much more, on the philosophical problems of parapsychology, see Flew 1987.)

(iii) Especially since the seventies there has been a revival of interest in and a considerable expansion of the study of near death experiences (NDEs), especially those describable as out of the body experiences (OBEs). For instance: R. A. Moody's *Life after Life* (1977) and J. C. Hampe's *To Die is Gain* (1972) have both sold well and attracted the attention of the electronic media. Paul and Linda Badham round off their very creditably critical account of the research reports of these and other writers with the question: 'If we accept these "traveller's tales" from the dying as evidential, what conclusions follow?' Their own cautious conclusion about the OBEs among the NDEs is: 'if no other plausible explanation can be put forward, then we have some grounds for accepting them as being what their percipients claim them to be – reports of what actually happens at the moment of death. And what appears to happen is that the soul leaves the body and begins to move on to another mode of existence' (1982, p. 89).

For us the immediate interest is in the prior question whether any sort of NDEs do or would support, as the Badhams clearly believe, a Platonic–Cartesian view of the nature of man. It is only if that is answered in the affirmative that there arises, as here logically secondary, the question whether they do or would constitute evidence for survival. The prior question itself arises because many people have reported that, usually in the crisis period of a serious illness, it has seemed to them that they were seeing themselves from a point of view, often a moving point of view, other than that occupied by their own eyes, and probably while their eyes were in any case shut. They have seemed to see, and much more rarely in other modes to perceive, both themselves lying apparently unconscious in their beds and other objects not visible or otherwise sensible from the position of those beds.

It is said too that sometimes the subjects of these OBEs produce information, which appears to them to have been sensibly acquired, about objects not normally observable, even by the medical staff and fit visitors (P. and L. Badham 1982, pp. 74–5).

Certainly these are very odd and very remarkable experiences. Nor is there any reasonable doubt but that they do occur; although whether any of their subjects can in fact produce information about objects not normally observable is much more open to question. But, whereas we cannot deny the occurrence of private experiences save at the price of denying the good faith of the subjects reporting such experiences, we can and must challenge most of the interpretations usually put upon these experiences.

The fact that they undoubtedly do occur, albeit rarely, is no more a reason for saying that the person having such experiences is at the time disembodied, than is the fact that we can all image ongoings distant in either time or place a reason for saying that, when we are engaged in these imagings, we are actually then or there, rather than when and where we in fact are. And, if subjects do produce information about objects not normally observable by anyone, then, as in the seance room situation, these achievements can and should be most economically described in terms of the psi-powers of those subjects, with the assistance perhaps of some unwitting collaborators.

The case of OBEs can for present philosophical if not for psychological purposes be assimilated to that of imagination (imaging). For what is in dispute is not what experiences are had or what images are formed, but how these experiences and these images are properly to be described. So, just as the correct answer to the question 'Where and when is the woman imagining she is Helen of Troy, being seduced by Paris?', is 'Wherever she is when she is doing the imagining; maybe in boring Bootle on a wet Sunday afternoon!'; so the answer to the question 'Where was the patient when he was having out of the body experiences?', is – just as dispiritingly – 'In his bed, apparently unconscious.'

The case of the British naval hero Lord Nelson is similar, but not the same. He took the fact that he sometimes suffered twinges where the arm lost in battle should have been as evidence that there are, and we are, incorporeal souls. Since these twinges undoubtedly fell into the category of bodily sensations, they surely constitute evidence, if anything, for astral bodies rather than for incorporeal souls. But, waiving that point, suppose that Nelson, or those other amputees known to Descartes in his soldier days, had reported itches and throbs as felt not where their limbs should have been but way out of the body – say on the other side of the public bar. This would still be no justification for holding that they themselves were on that other side, and not wherever they in fact were. I may feel a sensation, just as I may imagine something, as here or there or anywhere. But I myself am wherever I am having the feeling, or doing the imagining (imaging).

3   What would bodilessness be like, and for whom or what?

Back in section 2 of chapter seven it was suggested that, while it must surely be self-contradictory to ask what it would be like *for me* to be disembodied, it may not be similarly senseless to ask what it would be like, not *for me* as a person – a mature organism of the species Homo sapiens – but for a specimen of a hypothetical, grossly alien, yet still perhaps coherently describable form of existence if not of life – a bodiless rational being – to be a bodiless rational being. It was also noticed there that those who have raised this question – usually in the first, rejected form – have normally been negligent in their reluctance to think it through. By far the most exhaustive effort to be found in the parapsychological literature is an article entitled 'Survival and the Idea of "Another World"' (Price 1965).

   This article urges: 'Surely it is easy enough to conceive . . . that experiences might occur after Jones' death, in such a way that his personal identity is preserved.' Assuming that this is conceded, Price proceeds at once to state what he expects will be the main objection: 'But, it will be said, the idea of after-death *experiences* is just the difficulty. What kind of experiences could they conceivably be?' (p.3). His answer is that the next world might be a Berkeleyan Universe, consisting of nothing else but bodiless beings having Berkeleyan ideas. But, unlike Berkeley, Price makes what he hopes will be adequate provision for the possibility of knowledge of, and even acquaintance with, other people: 'There is no reason why an image-world should not contain a number of images which are telepathic apparitions; and, if it did, one could quite intelligently speak of 'meeting other persons' in such a world' (p. 11).

Already in earlier chapters sufficient has been said to show that we cannot grant what Price assumes will be granted. Prior to the difficulty to which he devotes most of his considerable ingenuity there is another and more fundamental. Before any question can arise about the object or content of any experiences there has to be some subject to which these experiences are attributed. Nor can it be admitted that, not being a person at all, a Humian collection of 'loose and separate' experiences could be the same person as our deceased friend Jones. But the fresh question to press is whether such a bodiless being could be a rational agent.

In order to fill this bill our bodiless being must be able both to acquire information from, and to make changes in, its environment. Information is needed both in deciding where the force is to be directed and to check whether the intended change has in fact been effected: 'Action and perception are in this way necessarily complementary and cannot be assimilated to each other' (Hampshire 1959, p. 52).

But now, a bodiless being cannot effect changes by applying pressures from parts or the whole of its body. Because that is precisely what it has not got and is not. So if it is to do anything at all it will only be by exercising powers of psychokinesis. These powers, however, cannot be directed on the basis of information supplied by the senses. For any bodiless being must lack sense-organs and, hence, senses. So if its activities are to be rationally directed, then that can only be upon the basis of information supplied by psi-gamma.

Among those who believe that they have given sense to talk of incorporeal spirits and disembodied persons it appears to be universally assumed that such beings could be said to acquire and to transmit information, and to know that they had acquired and transmitted information, by what these people will certainly be thinking of as Extra-Sensory Perception (ESP). In so far as they have recognized a problem about how such beings might act, they have presumably also taken it that their actions would be both directed upon the basis of information supplied by ESP and effected by exercises of PK; these last themselves identified as such by further exercises of ESP. The idea has been that these bodiless beings would both acquire and transmit information directly 'by telepathy', both from and to members of their own kind and from and to flesh and blood persons; and also acquire information, equally directly, 'by clairvoyance' from the ordinarily sensible world of non-personal things.

Apart from the present writer no one seems to have drawn a crucial corollary from the fact that psi-gamma at present is – and it would appear can only be – so defined as to be identifiable through nothing else but subsequent sensory check-ups. Suppose for a moment that there were such incorporeal subjects of experience. And suppose further that there was from time to time a close correspondence between the mental contents of two of these beings; although such a fact could not, surely, be known by any normal means to anyone in either our world or the next? Now, how could either of these two souls have, indeed how could there be, any good reason for hypothesizing the existence of the other; or of any others? How could such beings have, indeed how could there be, any good reason for picking out some of their own mental contents as – so to speak – messages received; and for taking these but not those to be, not expressions of a spontaneous and uncontrolled exercise of the imagination, but externally provoked communication input? Suppose these two challenging questions could be answered. Still the third would be, in an aptly Berkeleyan phrase, 'the killing blow'. For how could such beings identify and particular items as correspondently true or correspondently false, or even give sense to this distinction?

The upshot seems to be: that the concept of psi-gamma is essentially parasitical upon everyday, this-wordly notions; so that, where there could not be perception, there could not be 'extra-sensory perception' either. It is, as we have seen, too often and too easily assumed that psi-capacities not only could be, but would have to be, the attributes of something immaterial and incorporeal; mainly for no better reason than that they would be non-physical in the quite different sense of being outwith the scope of today's physical theories. Yet the truth is that the very concepts of psi are just as much involved with the human body as are those of all other distinctively human (and much more certainly applicable) human concepts. In the gnomic words quoted in an earlier chapter: 'The human body is the best picture of the human soul' (Wittgenstein 1953, p. 178).

Bibliography

This includes all those works mentioned in the text, but is not intended to cover other works. Where the date is given in square brackets it is that of original publication (and that of the first publication in the original language in the case of translations). A date given in parentheses in such entries, or for a 'classical' text, is that of a modern, or translated, edition. In the text no dates are given for classical texts except where there is a specific page reference. All page references are to the modern editions listed in the Bibliography, even if the text reference date is that of original publication (in which case it is given in square brackets).

Abelson, R. (1977) *Persons* (London: Macmillan).

Anscombe, G. E. M. (1981) *The Collected Philosophical Papers of G. E. M. Anscombe* (Oxford: Blackwell).

Anstey, F. (1887) *Vice-Versa* (London: Smith, Elder; revised edn).

Aquinas, St Thomas (1951) *Aristotle's de anima in the Version of William of Moerbeke and the Commentary of St Thomas Aquinas* (1951), translated by K. Foster and S. Humphries (London: Routledge and Kegan Paul).

Aquinas, St Thomas (1984) *Questions on the Soul*. Translated and introduced by J. H. Robb (Milwaukee, WI: Marquette UP).

Aristophanes (1950) All the plays are available in the Loeb Classical Library, with translations by B. B. Rogers, revised edn, published in London by Heinemann and in Cambridge MA by Harvard UP.

Aristotle (1907) *de anima* [On the Soul]. Text, translation and editorial material by R. D. Hicks (Cambridge: CUP).

Aristotle (1926) *Nicomachean Ethics*, translated by H. Rackham (London, and New York: Heinemann, and Putnam).

Armstrong, D. M. (1968) *A Materialist Theory of the Mind* (London: Routledge and Kegan Paul).

Arnauld, A. [1662] *The Art of Thinking* (now always known as the *Port-Royal Logic*), translated by J. Dickoff and P. James (Indianapolis: Bobbs-Merrill, 1964).

Augustine, St, of Hippo (1945) *The City of God*, translated by J. Healey, edited by R. V. G. Tasker (London, and New York: Dent, and Dutton).

Augustine, St, of Hippo (1919) *Confessions*, translated by W. Watts (London, and Cambridge, MA: Heinemann, and Harvard UP).

Augustine, St, of Hippo (1961) *The Enchiridion on Faith, Hope and Love*, translated by F. J. Shaw, edited by H. Paolucci (Chicago: Regnery Gateway).

Ayer, A. J. (1940) *The Foundations of Empirical Knowledge* (London: Macmillan).

Ayer, A. F. (1946) *Language, Truth and Logic* (London: Gollancz; 2nd edn).

Ayer, A. J. (1973) *The Central Questions of Philosophy* (London: Weidenfeld and Nicolson).

Badham, P. and L. (1982) *Immortality or Extinction* (London: Macmillan).

Baier, K. (1965) 'Action and agent', *Monist*, XLIX (2), 183–95.

Behan, D. P. (1979) 'Locke on persons and personal identity', *Canadian Journal of Philosophy* (March).

Beloff, J. (1963) Presidential Address, *Journal of the Society for Psychical Research*, XLII, 101–16.

Beloff, J. (1965) 'The identity hypothesis: a critique', in J. R. Smythies (ed.), *Brain and Mind* (London: Routledge and Kegan Paul).

Berkeley, G. (1901) *Works*, edited by A. C. Fraser (Oxford: Clarendon).

Boore, B. N. (1981) *The Philosophical Possibilities beyond Death* (Springfield, IL: C. C. Thomas).

Borst, C. V. (ed.) (1970) *The Mind/Brain Identity Theory* (London: Macmillan).

Bradley, F. H. (1876) *Ethical Studies* (London: Henry King).

Bradley, F. H. (1897) *Appearance and Reality* (London, and New York: Sonnenschein, and Macmillan; 2nd edn).

Bradley, F. H. (1935) *Collected Essays* (Oxford: Clarendon).

Broad, C. D. (1925) *The Mind and its Place in Nature* (London: Kegan Paul, Trench, Trubner).

Broad, C. D. (1930) *Five Types of Ethical Theory* (London: Kegan Paul, Trench, Trubner).

Broad, C. D. (1962) *Lectures on Psychical Research* (New York: Humanities).
Bullock, A. and Stalybrass, O. (eds) (1977) *The Fontana Dictionary of Modern Thought* (London: Collins Fontana).
Butler, J. (1896) *Butler's Works*, edited by W. E. Gladstone (Oxford: Clarendon).
Butterfield, H. (1951) *The Origins of Modern Science* (London: G. Bell).
Campbell, K. (1970) *Body and Mind* (London: Macmillan).
Carroll, L. [1865] *Alice's Adventures in Wonderland*, in *The Complete Works of Lewis Carroll* (London: Nonesuch, 1939).
Carroll, L. [1872] *Through the Looking Glass*, in ibid.
Chandler, R. (1949) *Farewell, My Lovely* (Harmondsworth: Penguin).
Cicero, M. T. (1967) *de natura deorum*, translated by H. Rackham (London, and Cambridge, MA: Heinemann, and Harvard UP).
Coard, B. (1971) *How the West Indian child is made educationally sub-normal in the British School System* (London: New Beacon).
Collingwood, R. G. (1940) *An Essay on Metaphysics* (Oxford: Clarendon).
Cottingham, J. G. (1978a) 'A brute to the brutes', *Philosophical Quarterly*.
Cottingham, J. G. (1978b) 'Descartes on "Thought"', *Philosophical Quarterly*.
Cottingham, J. G. (1986) *Descartes* (Oxford: Blackwell).
Coval, S. (1966) *Scepticism and the First Person* (London: Methuen).
Dennett, D. (1976) 'Conditions of personhood', in Rorty 1976.
Descartes, R. (1934) *The Philosophical Works*, translated by E. S. Haldane and G. R. T. Ross (Cambridge: CUP).
Diderot, D. (1978) *Oeuvres complètes*, edited by J. Varloot (Paris: Hermann).
Diels, H. (1954) *Die Fragmente der Vorsokratiker*, edited by W. Krantz (Berlin: Weidmannsche; 7th edn).
Dodds, E. R. (1932) 'Why I do not believe in survival', in *Proceedings of the Society for Psychical Research*, XLII; reprinted in Flew 1987, V. 9.
Douglas, A. H. (1910) *Pietro Pomponazzi* (Cambridge: CUP).
Ducasse, C. J. (1961) *Belief in Life after Death* (Springfield, IL: C. C. Thomas).
Ducasse, C. J. (1962) 'What would constitute conclusive evidence of survival after death?', *Journal of the Society for Psychical Research*, XLI.
Dumont, F. (1959) *After Life in Roman Paganism* (New York: Dover).

Feigl, H. (1958) 'The "mental" and the "physical"', in Feigl et al. 1958.

Feigl, H., Scriven, M. and Maxwell, G. (1958) *Minnesota Studies in the Philosophy of Science* (Minneapolis: Minnesota UP).

Flew, Annis (1953) 'Images, supposing and imagining', *Philosophy* (July).

Flew, A. G. N. (1950a) '"Selves"', *Mind*.

Flew, A. G. N. (1950b) 'Theology and Falsification', first published in *University* (Oxford), reprinted in over thirty places, including Flew 1976a.

Flew, A. G. N. (1951a) 'Death', first published in *University* (Oxford) in 1951; reprinted in Flew and MacIntyre 1956 but – unlike Flew 1950b – nowhere else. Most of its contents were, however, broadcast within the framework of the BBC Third Programme discussion on 'The Question of a Future Life'.

Flew, A. G. N. (1951b) 'Locke and the Problem of Personal Identity', in *Philosophy*. This was reprinted in revised verions: both in C. B. Martin and D. M. Armstrong (eds) (1968) *Locke and Berkeley* (New York: Doubleday); and in B. Brody (ed.) (1974) *Readings in the Philosophy of Religion* (Englewood Cliffs, NJ: Prentice-Hall); also in Flew 1976a.

Flew, A. G. N. (1953) *A New Approach to Psychical Research* (London: C. A. Watts).

Flew, A. G. N. (1954) 'Could an effect precede its cause?', *Proceedings of the Aristotelian Society*, Supp. vol. XXVIII.

Flew, A. G. N. (1956a) 'Can a man witness his own funeral?', *Hibbert Journal*; reprinted in J. Feinberg (ed.) (1971) *Reason and Responsibility* (Belmont, CA: Dickenson); in W. J. Blackstone (ed.) (1972) *Meaning and Existence* (New York: Holt, Rinehart and Winston); in F. A. Westphal (ed.) (1972) *The Art of Philosophy* (Englewood Cliffs, NJ: Prentice-Hall); and in P. A. French (ed.) (1975) *Exploring Philosophy* (Morristown, NJ: General Learning Press). P. A. French (1975) also includes a remarkably similar piece under his own name in another of his collections, *Philosophers in Wonderland* (Saint Paul, MN: Llewelyn). There is also a revised version in Flew 1976a.

Flew, A. G. N. (1956b) 'Facts and imagination', *Mind*.

Flew, A. G. N. (1958) 'Determinism and validity again', *Rationalist Annual*.

Flew, A. G. N. (1959) 'Determinism and rational behaviour', *Mind*.

Flew, A. G. N. (1961) *Hume's Philosophy of Belief* (London, and New York: Routledge and Kegan Paul, and Humanities).

Flew, A. G. N. (1963a) 'The Platonic presuppositions of the survival hypothesis', *Journal of the Society for Psychical Research*, XLII.

Flew, A. G. N. (1963b) 'The Soul of Mr A. M. Quinton', *Journal of Philosophy*.

Flew, A. G. N. (ed.) (1964) *Body, Mind and Death* (New York: Collier-Macmillan).

Flew, A. G. N. (1966) *God and Philosophy* (London: Hutchinson); reissued in 1984 as *God: A Critical Enquiry* by Open Court of La Salle, IL.

Flew, A. G. N. (1971) *An Introduction to Western Philosophy* (London, and Indianapolis: Thames and Hudson, and Bobbs-Merrill).

Flew, A. G. N. (1972) 'Is there a case for disembodied survival?', *Journal of the American Society for Psychical Research*; reprinted in J. M. O. Wheatley and H. L. Edge (eds) (1976) *Philosophical Dimensions in Parapsychology* (Springfield, IL: C. C. Thomas); also, in a revised version, in Flew 1976a.

Flew, A. G. N. (1973a) *Crime or Disease?* (London: Macmillan).

Flew, A. G. N. (1973b) 'The question of survival', in T. Penelhum (ed.), *Immortality* (Belmont, CA: Wadsworth). This was a revised version of Flew 1953, ch. VII.

Flew, A. G. N. (1974) 'Was Berkeley a precursor of Wittgenstein?', in W. B. Todd (ed.), *Hume and the Enlightenment* (Edinburgh: Edinburgh UP).

Flew, A. G. N. (1975) *Thinking about Thinking* (London: Collins Fontana). This is marketed in the USA, by Prometheus of Buffalo, NY, as *Thinking Straight*.

Flew, A. G. N. (1976a) *The Presumption of Atheism* (London: Elek/Pemberton); reissued in 1984 as *God, Freedom and Immortality* by Prometheus of Buffalo, NY.

Flew, A. G. N. (1976b) *Sociology, Equality and Education* (London: Macmillan).

Flew, A. G. N. (1978) *A Rational Animal* (Oxford: Clarendon).

Flew, A. G. N. (1980) 'Parapsychology: science or pseudo-science?', *Pacific Philosophical Quarterly*; reprinted in M. P. Hanen, J. J. Osler and R. G. Weyant (eds) (1980) *Science, Pseudo-Science and Society* (Waterloo, Ontario: Wilfrid Laurier UP); in P. Grim (ed.), *The Occult, Science and Philosophy* (Albany, NY: SUNY Press, 1982); and in Kurtz 1986.

Flew, A. G. N. (1982) 'A strong programme for the sociology of belief', *Inquiry* (Oslo).

Flew, A. G. N. (1983) ' "Freedom is Slavery": a slogan for our new philosopher kings', in A. P. Griffiths (ed.), *Of Liberty* (Cambridge: CUP).

Flew, A. G. N. (1984) *Darwinian Evolution* (London: Paladin).

Flew, A. G. N. (1985) 'The burden of proof', in L. S. Rouner (ed.) *Knowing Religiously* (Notre Dame, IN: Notre Dame UP).

Flew, A. G. N. (1986a) *Hume: Philosopher of Moral Science* (Oxford: Blackwell).

Flew, A. G. N. (1986b) 'An ungodly muddle', *Encounter* (September), 74–6.

Flew, A. G. N. (ed.) (1987) *Readings in the Philosophy of Parapsychology* (Buffalo, NY: Prometheus).

Flew, A. G. N. and MacIntyre, A. C. (eds) (1956) *New Essays in Philosophical Theology* (London: Student Christian Movement Press).

Flew, A. G. N. and Vesey, G. (1987) *Agency and Necessity* (Oxford: Blackwell).

Freeman, D. (1983) *Margaret Mead and Samoa* (Cambridge, MA: Harvard UP).

Gallie, I. (1936) 'Is the self a substance?', *Mind*.

Geach, P. T. (1969) *God and the Soul* (London: Routledge and Kegan Paul).

Geach, P. T. (1977) *The Virtues* (Cambridge: CUP).

Greig, J. Y. T. (ed.) (1932) *The Letters of David Hume* (Oxford: Clarendon).

Grice, P. (1941) 'Personal Identity', *Mind*.

Hall, T. H. (1962) *The Spiritualists* (London: Duckworth).

Hall, T. H. (1964) *The Strange Case of Edmund Gurney* (London: Duckworth).

Hall, T. H. (1965) *New Light on Old Ghosts* (London: Duckworth).

Hall, T. H. (1984) *The Enigma of Daniel Home* (Buffalo, NY: Prometheus).

Hall, T. H. (1985) *The Medium and the Scientist* (Buffalo, NY: Prometheus).

Hamlyn D. (1984) *Metaphysics* (Cambridge: CUP).

Hampe, J. C. (1972) *To Die is Gain*, translated by M. Kohl (London: Darton, Longman and Todd).

Hampshire, S. N. (1959) *Thought and Action* (London: Chatto and Windus).

Hare, R. M. (1971) *Essays on Philosophical Method* (London: Macmillan).

Hepburn, R. W. (1963) 'From world to God', *Mind*, LXXII.
Hobbes, T. (1961) *The English Works of Thomas Hobbes*, edited by Sir William Molesworth (London, 1839; reprinted Oxford, 1961).
Hofstadter, D. R. and Dennett, D. C. (1981) *The Mind's I* (New York: Basic).
Holland, R. F. (1961) Review of Martin 1959, *Mind*.
Housman, A. E. (1931) *Juvenalis Saturae* (Cambridge: CUP; revised edn).
Hume, D. [1739–40] *Treatise of Human Nature*, edited by L. A. Selby-Bigge, revised by P. H. Nidditch (Oxford: Clarendon; 2nd edn, 1978).
Hume, D. [1742–77] *Essays Moral Political and Literary* edited by E. F. Miller (Indianapolis: Liberty Classics, 1985).
Hume, D. [1748] *An Enquiry concerning Human Understanding*, in *Hume's Enquiries*, edited by L. A. Selby-Bigge, revised by P. H. Nidditch (Oxford: Clarendon; 3rd edn, 1975).
Huxley, T. H. (1915) *Elementary Physiology* (London: Macmillan; 6th edn).
Jerome, St (1910–61) *Sancti Eusebii Hieronymi opera*, edited by I. Hilberg and S. Reiter (Vienna: Tempsky).
Justin Martyr, St (1861) 'Dialogue with Trypho', in *Works*, edited and translated by G. T. Davie (Oxford: Parker).
Kafka, F. [1916] *Metamorphosis, and Other Stories*, translated by W. and E. Muir (Harmondsworth: Penguin, 1961).
Kaufmann, W. (1959) *Critique of Religion and Philosophy* (London: Faber).
Kenny, A. (1970) *Descartes: Philosophical Letters* (Oxford: Blackwell).
Kenny, A. (1973) *The Anatomy of the Soul* (Oxford: Blackwell).
Koran, The. Translated by N. J. Dawood (Harmondsworth: Penguin, 1956).
Kripke, S. (1980) *Naming and Necessity* (Cambridge, MA: Harvard UP).
Kurtz, P. (ed.) (1986) *A Skeptic's Handbook of Parapsychology* (Buffalo, NY: Prometheus).
Leibniz, G. W. [1684] *Reflections on Knowledge, Truth and Ideas*, in P. P. Wiener (ed.) (1951) *Leibniz Selections* (New York: Scribner).
Levin, M. (1979) *Metaphysics and the Mind–Body Problem* (Oxford: Clarendon).
Lewis, C. S. (1960) *Miracles: A Preliminary Study* (London: Collins Fontana; revised edn).
Lewis, H. D. (1973) *The Self and Immortality* (London: Macmillan).
Lewis, H. D. (1978) *Persons and Life after Death* (London: Macmillan).

192		*Bibliography*

Lewy, C. (1942–3) 'Is the notion of disembodied existence self-contradictory?', *Proceedings of the Aristotelian Society*.

Lippman, W. (1931) *A Preface to Morals* (New York: Macmillan).

Locke, J. [1690] *An Essay concerning Human Understanding*, edited by P. H. Nidditch (Oxford; Clarendon, 1975).

Lovejoy, A. O. (1936) *The Great Chain of Being* (Cambridge, MA: Harvard UP).

Lucretius, T. (1947) *de rerum natura* translated by W. H. D. Rouse (London, and Cambridge MA: Heinemann, and Harvard UP).

McDougall, W. (1911) *Body and Mind: A History and a Defense of Animism* (London: Methuen).

Mace, C. A. (1942–3) 'Concerning imagination', *Proceedings of the Aristotelian Society*.

Mackie, J. L. (1982) *The Miracle of Theism* (Oxford: Clarendon).

M'Taggart, J. M. E. (1906) *Some Dogmas of Religion* (London: Edward Arnold).

M'Taggart, J. M. E. (1915) *Human Immortality and Preexistence* (London: Edward Arnold). This was a residue of chapters III and IV of M'Taggart 1906, with a timely Postscript proclaiming that the author had since 'become more firmly convinced that the nature of reality can be shown to be such as to justify a belief both in immortality and in preexistence.'

Martin, C. B. (1959) *Religious Belief* (Ithaca, NY: Cornell UP).

Medvedev, Z. (1979) *Nuclear Disaster in the Urals* (London: Angus and Robertson).

Milne, A. A. (1926) *Winnie-the-Pooh* (London: Methuen).

Milne, A. A. (1928) *The House at Pooh Corner* (London: Methuen).

Milton, J. (n.d.) *Milton: Complete Poetry and Selected Prose*, edited by E. H. Visiak (London: Nonesuch).

Moody, R. A. (1977) *Life after Life* (New York: Bantam).

Myers, F. W. H. (1902) *Human Personality and its Survival of Bodily Death* (London: Longmans Green).

Nagel, T. (1974) 'What is it like to be a bat?', *Philosophical Review*; reprinted in Hofstadter and Dennett 1981.

Parfit, D. (1971) 'Personal identity', *Philosopical Review*.

Parfitt, D. (1986) *Reasons and Persons* (Oxford: OUP).

Passmore, J. A. (1952) *Hume's Intentions* (Cambridge: CUP).

Péguy, C. (1957) *Oeuvres en prose*, edited by M. Péguy (Paris: Gallimard).

Peirce, C. S. (1931–5) *Collected papers*, edited by C. Hartshorne and P. Weiss (Cambridge, MA: Harvard UP).

Penelhum, T. (1970) *Survival and Disembodied Existence* (London: Routledge and Kegan Paul).

Penelhum, T. (1985) *Butler* (London: Routledge and Kegan Paul).

Perry, J. (ed.) (1975) *Personal Identity* (Berkeley, CA: California UP).

Perry, J. (1976) 'The importance of being identical', in Rorty 1976.

Phillips, D. Z. (1970) *Death and Immortality* (London: Macmillan).

Plato All the dialogues are available in the Loeb Classical Library, with translations by various hands, published jointly in London by Heinemann and in Cambridge, MA by Harvard UP. The translations in the text above are for the most part my own.

Popper, K. R. (1979) *Objective Knowledge* (Oxford: Clarendon; revised edn).

Popper, K. R. (1982) *The Open Universe: An Argument for Indeterminism* (London: Hutchinson).

Popper, K. R. and Eccles, J. C. (1977) *The Self and Its Brain* (Berlin, New York and London: Springer International).

Presley, C. F. (ed.) (1967) *The Identity Theory of Mind* (St Lucia, Queensland: Queensland UP).

Price, H. H. (1940) 'The permanent value of Hume's philosophy', *Philosophy*.

Price, H. H. (1965) 'Survival and the idea of "another world"', first published in the *Proceedings of the Society for Psychical Research*, but more easily in Smythies 1965.

Price, H. H. (1972) *Essays in the Philosophy of Religion* (Oxford: Clarendon).

Pringle-Pattison, A. S. (1922) *The Idea of Immortality* (Oxford: Clarendon).

Puccetti, R. (1968) *Persons: A Study of Possible Moral Agents in the Universe* (London: Macmillan).

Quinton, A. M. (1962) 'The soul', *Journal of Philosophy*, LIX (15).

Reid, T. [1785] *Essays on the Intellectual Powers of Man*, edited and abridged by A. D. Woozley (London: Macmillan, 1941).

Rhine, J. B. (1937) *New Frontiers of the Mind* (New York: Farmer and Rinehart).

Rhine, J. B. (1948) *The Reach of the Mind* (London: Faber).

Rorty, A. O. (ed.) (1976) *The Identities of Persons* (Berkeley, CA: California UP).

Russell, B. A. W. [1911] *The Problems of Philosophy* (London: OUP, 1967).

Russell, B. A. W. (1921) *The Analysis of Mind* (London: Allen and Unwin).

Russell, B. A. W. (1922) *Our Knowledge of the External World* (London: Allen and Unwin).

Ryle, G. (1949) *The Concept of Mind* (London: Hutchinson).

Ryle, G. (1950) 'The physical basis of mind', in P. Laslett (ed.) *The Physical Basis of Mind* (Oxford: Blackwell).

Ryle, G. (1954) *Dilemmas* (Cambridge: CUP).

Santayana, G. [1926] *Reason in Religion* (New York: Collier, 1962).

Schlick, M. (1937) 'Meaning and verification', *Philosophical Review* for July 1937, reprinted in H. Feigl and W. Sellars (eds) (1949) *Readings in Philosophical Analysis* (New York: Appleton-Century-Crofts).

Sherrington, C. (1940) *Man on his Nature* (Cambridge: CUP).

Shoemaker, S. (1963) *Self-Knowledge and Self-Identity* (Ithaca, NY: Cornell UP).

Shoemaker, S. (1984) Contributions to S. Shoemaker and R. Swinburne, *Personal Identity* (Oxford: Blackwell).

Sidgwick, H. (1874) *The Methods of Ethics* (London: Macmillan).

Skinner, B. F. (1948) *Walden Two* (New York: Macmillan).

Skinner, B. F. (1971) *Beyond Freedom and Dignity* (New York, and London: Knopf, and Cape).

Smart, J. J. C. (1959) 'Sensations and brain processes', first published in the *Philosophical Review*; and reprinted, in variously revised versions, many times; among others in Borst 1970.

Smythies, F. R. (ed.) (1965) *Brain and Mind* (London: Routledge and Kegan Paul).

Sterling, C. (1982) *The Masaryk Case* (Boston: Godine).

Stevenson, I. (1966) *Twenty Cases Suggestive of Reincarnation* (Charlottesville, VA. Virginia UP).

Strawson, P. F. (1958) 'Persons', in Feigl et al. 1958.

Strawson, P. F. (1959) *Individuals* (London: Methuen).

Swinburne, R. (1977) *The Coherence of Theism* (Oxford: Clarendon).

Swinburne, R. (1984) Contributions to S. Shoemaker and R. Swinburne, *Personal Identity* (Oxford: Blackwell).

Swinburne, R. (1986) *The Evolution of the Soul* (Oxford: OUP).

Teichman, J. (1985) 'The definition of person', *Philosophy*.

Tertullian (1870) *de anima*, in *Writings of Tertullian*, translated by P. Holmes (Edinburgh: T. and T. Clark), vol. II.

Tillich, P. (1968) *Systematic Theology* (Welwyn, Herts.: Nisbet).

Vesey, G. (1974) *Personal Identity* (London: Macmillan).

Waismann, F. (1951) 'Verifiability', in A. G. N. Flew (ed.), *Logic and Language: First Series* (Oxford: Blackwell).

Waley, A. (1918) *170 Chinese Poems* (London: Constable).

Ward, J. (1911) *The Realm of Ends* (Cambridge: CUP).

Williams, B. (1956) 'Personal identity and individuation', *Proceedings of the Aristotelian Society*; reprinted in Williams 1973.

Williams, B. (1966) 'Imagination and the Self', a British Academy Annual Philosophical Lecture; reprinted in Williams 1973.

Williams, B. (1973) *Problems of the Self* (Cambridge. CUP).

Wisdom, J. (1952) *Other Minds* (Oxford: Blackwell).

Wisdom, J. (1953) *Philosophy and Psychoanalysis* (Oxford: Blackwell).

Wittgenstein, L. [1921] *Tractatus Logico-Philosophicus*, translated by C. K. Ogden (London: Kegan Paul, Trench, Trubner, 1922).

Wittgenstein, L. (1953) *Philosophical Investigations*, translated by G. E. M. Anscombe (Oxford: Blackwell).

Wittgenstein, L. (1958) *The Blue and Brown Books* (Oxford: Blackwell).

Name Index